Gender and Economic Growth
in Tanzania

Gender and Economic Growth in Tanzania

Creating Opportunities for Women

Amanda Ellis
Mark Blackden
Jozefina Cutura
Fiona MacCulloch
Holger Seebens

THE WORLD BANK
Washington, D.C.

1 2 3 4 5 10 09 08 07

ISBN-13:   978-0-8213-7262-3
eISBN-13:   978-0-8213-7262-0
DOI: 10.1596/978-0-8213-7262-3

Cover photo: Batik design created in Arusha Town, Tanzania.

Library of Congress Cataloging-in-Publication Data

Gender and economic growth in Tanzania : unleashing the power of women.
    p. cm.
Includes bibliographical references and index.
ISBN 978-0-8213-7262-3—ISBN 978-0-8213-7263-0 (electronic)
1. Women in development—Tanzania. 2. Women—Government policy—Tanzania. 3. Women—Tanzania—Social conditions. 4. Women—Tanzania—Economic conditions. 5. Business women—Tanzania. I. World Bank.

    HQ1240.5.T34G464 2007
    338.96780082–dc22   2007022881

Contents

Boxes

Figures

Tables

Foreword

Although much of African economic activity is in the hands of women, especially in agriculture and informal business, economic opportunities are often markedly different for men and women. Creating opportunities for women can help not only to empower women, but also to unlock the full economic potential of their nations.

Gender and Economic Growth in Tanzania was undertaken at the request of the Ministry of Industry, Trade, and Marketing, cognizant of the need to ensure that government policies and regulations result in practical benefits for women entrepreneurs. The report was carried out by the IFC Gender Entrepreneurship Markets (GEM) program, the IFC Investment Climate Team for Africa, and the World Bank. Generous support was provided by the Bank-Netherlands Partnership Program (BNPP), the Canadian International Development Agency (CIDA), and the U.K Department for International Development (DFID). The report examines gender-based barriers in the business environment that limit women's contribution to the economy, and finds that Tanzania's economic growth and poverty reduction can be boosted by enabling women to contribute more fully to the goals of the country's National Strategy for Growth and Reduction of Poverty. A complementary *Voices of Women Entrepreneurs in Tanzania* publication profiles successful women business owners as role models, and offers a unique perspective, grounded in experience, on the obstacles and constraints they have had to overcome.

The two reports were formally launched in Tanzania in August 2007 in the presence of nearly 200 businesswomen, government officials, donors, and civil society representatives, whose continued support is essential for translating the study's recommendations into action.

The World Bank Group recognizes the critical importance of women's contribution to shared economic growth, especially in Africa. Through the new Gender Action Plan that focuses on "gender equality as smart economics," the organization is committed to act. FIAS, the multidonor investment climate advisory service of the World Bank Group, offers a comprehensive range of services tailored to governments' needs to help them improve their investment climate for domestic and foreign investment and to maximize the impact on poverty reduction. FIAS is committed to creating opportunities for women in business, as well as for men, and to integrating a gender perspective in its products and services. A deeper understanding of gender-based obstacles to business, as exemplified in this joint World Bank-FIAS-GEM series of *Gender and Economic Growth Assessments* (Uganda 2006, Ghana, 2007, Kenya 2007), is a practical result of that commitment, and feeds into advisory work to help client governments harness the full economic power of their entrepreneurs, regardless of gender. Tackling the gender-based obstacles to entrepreneurship analyzed in this report will not only enable women in Tanzania to make a fuller contribution to the economy and improve their families' livelihoods, but also help to create a business environment that is better for all enterprises in Tanzania.

Pierre Guislain
Director
Foreign Investment Advisory Service
World Bank Group

Acknowledgments

This assessment has been prepared by a team led by Amanda Ellis, and consisting of Mark Blackden, Jozefina Cutura, Fiona MacCulloch, and Holger Seebens, with inputs from Zahia-Lolila Ramin and Mary Agboli. The report was a collaborative effort, carried out by the International Finance Corporation's Gender Entrepreneurship Markets (IFC GEM) program, the Investment Climate Team for Africa, the World Bank and the U.K. Department for International Development (DFID).

The team has received considerable support and input from various women's organizations in the country, including the Tanzania Women's Chamber of Commerce, the Tanzania Women Lawyers Association, the Tanzania Association of Women Leaders in Agriculture and Environment, the Tanzania Media Women's Association, the Tanzania Gender Networking Program (TGNP), Tanzania Women Miners Association, the Federation of Associations of Women Entrepreneurs in Tanzania, and the Gender Macro Group.

We thank the Financial Sector Deepening Trust for sharing the data of their FinScope survey, and Julie Weeks for analyzing the data as input into the access to finance chapter. Valuable feedback on the report has been provided by Bede Lymo, Clare Manuel, Ian Robinson, Hagar Russ, Charles Rwechungura, Barbara Steenstrup and Michael Wong. The team also wishes to thank World Bank and IFC Tanzania country office staff, in particular, the World Bank Country Director at the time, Judy O'Connor, as well as Michael Wong and Elizabeth Massanja for their support during the team's fieldwork in Tanzania. We also thank IFC's regional manager, Jean-Philippe Prosper for his ongoing support.

We thank Tanzania's Ministry of Industry, Trade and Marketing for commissioning the report, particularly the Permanent Secretary, Dr. Stergomena Tax, as well as Jacqueline Maleko, Januarius Mrema, and Adiel Nyiti for their dedication and support of the project. In Zanzibar, we thank Mr. Affan Maalim, the Principal Secretary in the Ministry of Industry, Trade and Investments; Mr. Khalid Mohammed, the Principal Secretary in the Ministry of Labor, Youth, Women and Children Development; and Mr. Shabaan Said, of the Ministry of Industry, Trade, and Investments.

Several donors recognized as leaders in gender issues have generously supported this work, notably the Bank Netherlands Partnership Program (BNPP), the Canadian International Development Agency (CIDA), and DFID.

Finally, we wish to thank the wonderful women entrepreneurs of Tanzania and Zanzibar, whose enthusiasm and support continue to be an inspiration.

Ministerie van
Buitenlandse Zaken

Canadian   Agence
International   canadienne de
Development   développement
Agency   international

Canada

DFID Department for
      International
      Development

Abbreviations

BDS	Business development services
BEST	Business Environment Strengthening for Tanzania
BNPP	Bank Netherlands Partnership Program
BOT	Bank of Tanzania
BRELA	Business Registration and Licensing Agency
CEDAW	UN Convention of Elimination of all Forms of Discrimination Against Women
CIDA	Canadian International Development Agency
CTI	Confederation of Tanzania Industries
COSOTA	Copyright Society of Tanzania
CRC	UN Convention of the Rights of the Child
CRDB	Cooperative and Rural Development Bank
DFID	Department for International Development
DTIS	Diagnostic Trade Integration Study
EPZ	Export Processing Zone
FAWETA	Federation of Associations of Women Entrepreneurs in Tanzania
FIAS	Foreign Investment Advisory Service
FTZ	Free Trade Zone
IFC	International Finance Corporation

GDP	Gross domestic product
GEM	Gender Entrepreneurship Markets
ICA	Investment Climate Assessment
ICESCR	International Covenant on Economic, Social and Cultural Rights
ICRC	International Convention on the Rights of the Child
ILD	Institute for Liberty and Democracy
ILFS	Integrated Labor Force Survey
ILO	International Labour Organization
LMA	Law of Marriage Act, 1971
LRCT	Law Reform Commission of Tanzania
MDGs	Millennium Development Goals
MFC	Microfinance company
MFI	Microfinance institution
MKURABITA	Program to Formalise the Assets of the Poor of Tanzania and Strengthen the Rule of Law
MSE	Micro- and small-scale enterprise
MSME	micro, small, and medium enterprise
NDC	National Development Corporation
NETT	National Economic Partnership Agreement (EPA) Technical Team
NBS	National Bureau of Statistics
NMB	National Microfinance Bank
NSGRP	National Strategy for Growth and Reduction of Poverty
PAYE	Pay as you earn
PPA	Participatory Poverty Assessment
PSD	Private Sector Development
OSHA	Occupational Safety and Health Act
SACCO	Savings and Credit Cooperative Society
SEZ	Small Export Zones
SIDO	Small Industries Development Organization
SME	Small- and medium-size enterprise
TAWLA	Tanzania Women Lawyers Association
TAWLAE	Tanzania Association of Women Leaders in Agriculture and Environment
TAWOMA	Tanzania Women Miners Association
TGNP	Tanzania Gender Networking Program
TIN	Tax Identification Number
TLS	Tanganyika Law Society
TMP	Tax Modernisation Program

TPSF	Tanzania Private Sector Federation
TRA	Tanzania Revenue Authority
TRIPS	Trade Related Aspects of Intellectual Property Rights Agreement
TWCC	Tanzania Women's Chamber of Commerce
TWJA	Tanzanian Women Judges Association
UNCITRAL	United Nations Commission on International Trade Law
VAT	Value Added Tax
WED	Women Entrepreneurship Development Unit
WEDTF	Women's Entrepreneurship Development Fund
WGDP	Women and Gender Development Policy
WIPO	World Intellectual Property Organization
WTO	World Trade Organization
ZIPA	Zanzibar Investment Promotion Agency
ZRB	Zanzibar Revenue Board

Overview

Eliminating gender discrimination and empowering women are among the paramount challenges facing the world today. When women are healthy, educated and free to take the opportunities life affords them, children thrive and countries flourish, reaping a double dividend for women and children.

—Kofi A. Annan,
former Secretary-General of the United Nations (UNICEF 2007)

Background

Tanzania Has Been at the Forefront of Creating a Positive Legal Framework and Political Context for Gender Equality

Women's important contribution to economic activity in Tanzania is well recognized: In the 2006 World Economic Forum Global Gender Gap report Tanzania was ranked number 1 globally, out of 115 countries, in terms of women's economic participation.[1] Both government and civil society articulate the importance of gender equality, and numerous policies and strategies identify the need for continued progress. As part of its commitment to achieving the Millennium Development Goals (MDGs), especially MDG 3, relating to the empowerment of women, Tanzania has addressed gender issues in the following areas, all of which affect women's improved participation in the private sector:

- **Policy.** The *National Development Vision 2025* aims to attain "gender equality and the empowerment of women in all socio-economic and political relations and cultures." In 2000 Tanzania adopted a *Women and Gender Development Policy* (WGDP),[2] to ensure gender mainstreaming in all government policies, programs, and strategies.
- **Strategy.** The 2005 *National Strategy for Gender Development* specifies how gender mainstreaming is to be implemented (United Republic of Tanzania 2005b). In Zanzibar, the *Policy on the Protection and Development of Women* of 2001 provides a framework for promoting gender equality.
- **Ratification of international instruments.** Tanzania has ratified most major international human rights instruments, including Convention of Elimination of all Forms of Discrimination Against Women (CEDAW), International Covenant on Economic, Social and Cultural Rights (ICESCR), and International Convention on the Rights of the Child (ICRC), and has signed the African Political and the 1997 SADC Heads of States Declaration on Gender.
- **Constitutional reform.** Through a special amendment passed in 2000, discrimination on the basis of gender is prohibited under the constitution, which also protects the right of women to own land.
- **Legal reform.** Parliament has enacted a number of laws in support of women's economic and social well-being, including the Sexual Offences (Special Provisions) Act of 1998 and the two Land Acts of 1999, which established that women should be treated equally with men in terms of rights to acquire, hold, use, and deal with land. The Employment and Labor Relations Act of 2004 prohibited discrimination in the workplace on the basis of gender, required employers to promote equal opportunities, introduced maternity leave, and contained provisions protecting a mother's right to breastfeed and to be protected from engaging in hazardous employment.
- **Gender-responsive budgeting.** Gender budgeting processes are being institutionalized in all ministries, as well as regional and local authorities.
- **Political participation.** Affirmative action to include women in decision-making includes a recent act increasing the number of women's special seats in government (33 percent in local government councils and 20 percent in the Union Parliament); an increase in the participation of women in politics to 30 percent, in line with the SADC Declaration of

1997; and a recent act in Zanzibar increasing the number of women in the House of Representatives to 30 percent.

Certain Legal, Regulatory, and Administrative Barriers Still Hinder Women's Full Participation in Private Sector Development

This Gender and Growth Assessment (GGA) examines legal, regulatory, and administrative barriers to women's private sector participation in Tanzania. Building on intensive stakeholder consultations and the findings of numerous studies, notably the MKURABITA diagnostic (Institute for Liberty and Democracy 2005) and the 2003/4 Investment Climate Assessments for Tanzania and Zanzibar (World Bank 2004b, 2004c), this report examines gender-related barriers to growth and investment. It highlights legal and administrative constraints that have a disproportionately negative effect on female-headed businesses, and recommends needed reforms.

Culture and Traditional Norms Also Create Obstacles

Reforming the law and working to strengthen the institutional machinery for implementing gender goals are important, but cultural factors still strongly influence the ability of Tanzanian women to realize their potential in business. Cultural norms govern prevailing attitudes and beliefs. Not only do they include the subordination of women to men, but they also have a pervasive impact on social and economic life, and on how laws and regulations operate in practice.

Interviews conducted by the GGA team with Tanzanian women entrepreneurs in September and November 2006 reinforced the presence of culturally based obstacles to women's economic empowerment. The reluctance of husbands to allow their wives to engage in business activity, and time constraints due to competing domestic responsibilities were never far from the surface. These attitudes also impacted access to finance, as well as the ability to attend training and access to business development services. As a consequence, women's enterprises often remain precarious, usually tied to small-scale and informal activities that can be reconciled with their domestic obligations. This means that a substantial segment of Tanzania's entrepreneurial potential remains underexploited.

Addressing Gender Barriers Could Increase Economic Growth in Tanzania

Addressing gender barriers to women's participation in private sector would not only help unlock the full economic potential of women, but would help improve the environment for all businesses in Tanzania. Although Tanzania's economic growth has been strong, this report finds that if the country were to bring female secondary schooling and female total years of schooling to the same level as that now enjoyed by males, an additional annual percentage point of growth could be produced—a valuable contribution to achieving the 6–8 percent annual growth targets of the National Strategy for Growth and Reduction of Poverty (NSGRP or MKUKUTA).

Summary of Key Findings and Recommendations

Women play a substantial role in Tanzania's economy and are more active in agriculture, which accounts for 82 percent of the labor force. Of 17.8 million economically active people, 16.9 million are considered employed, and of these, women constitute 50.6 percent. The overall labor force participation rate (including the informal sector) of women is at 80.7 percent slightly higher than that of men (79.6 percent) (United Republic of Tanzania 2002a).

The distribution of men and women across the sectors is uneven: Women are slightly in the majority in agriculture (52 percent versus 48 percent) and in trade (55 percent versus 45 percent), whereas men dominate in manufacturing, construction, transport, and finance. The distribution of economic activity by type of employment is uneven too, showing important gender differences. Only 4.0 percent of employed women are in paid jobs, in either the formal or informal sector, compared with 9.8 percent of men (table 1), and a scant 2 percent of Tanzania's businesses operate legally (figure 1). Gender disparities are also evident in formal sector employment, where men account for 71 percent of workers. Men tend to be much better represented among regular waged employees than women. In the manufacturing sector where the waged employment rate is highest, only 18.6 percent of employees are women.

Table 1. Percentage of Currently Employed Persons, by Employment Status

Employment status	Current employment %			Female (Male = 100)
	Male	Female	Total	
Paid employment	9.8	4.0	6.9	40.8
Self-employment	8.9	7.8	8.3	87.6
Unpaid helper	3.0	4.6	3.8	153.3
Agriculture (own farm/shamba)	78.2	83.6	81.0	109.6
Total	100	100	100	

Source: Data from United Republic of tanzania (2002a), and staff calculations.

Figure 1. Percentages of Properties and Businesses Operating Extralegally in Tanzania

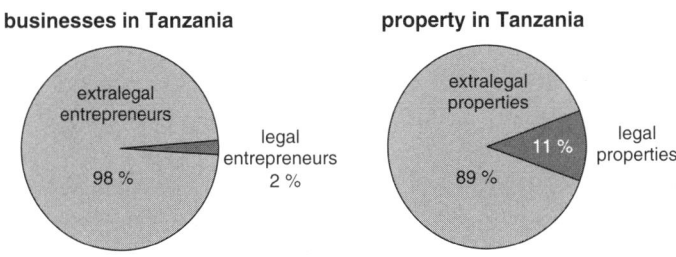

Source: Institute for Liberty and Democracy (2005).

Figure 2. Women's Participation in Tanzania's Economy

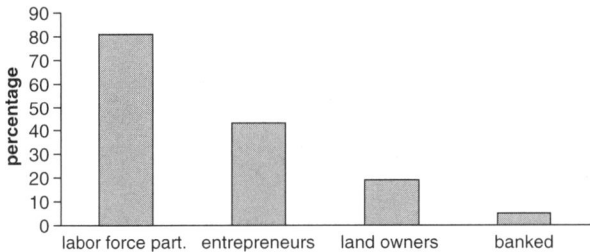

Source: National Bureau of Statistics (NBS) (2002); ILO (2005); IFAD (2005); FSDT (2007).

The National Bureau of Statistics (NBS) (2002) data show that in most paid labor occupations, men have substantially higher earnings compared with those of women. In manufacturing, the mean monthly income paid to women is TSh 42,413, which is almost 3.5 times lower than the average income earned by men. The ILO estimates that the number of women entrepreneurs ranges from 730,000 to 1.2 million (ILO 2003b). They are predominantly found in the micro, small, and medium enterprise (MSME) sector, where they are estimated to make up 43 percent of the total (figure 2) (IFAD 2005).

Reducing Bureaucratic Barriers

Barriers to establishing a business, particularly the lengthy and complex business registration, incorporation and licensing practices have a disproportionately negative effect on women, often making it impossible for them to get started. Tanzania's new Companies Act introduced a number of detailed changes to the regulation of companies. Yet the result of the reform is that complex and time-consuming requirements for company incorporation are perpetuated—costs which firms have an incentive to evade through informality (table 2). This incentive is even stronger for women entrepreneurs who tend to be more time and cash constrained than their male counterparts. Recommended reforms include the following:

- Introduce best practice models for company formation and operation that provide simplified, low-cost procedures and reporting requirements applicable to small companies.
- Fundamentally reform the Business Names (Registration) Act to remove the blanket requirement for registration.
- Design and implement a policy on sector licensing that (i) limits regulation strictly to areas where there is a clear necessity to preserve national security, key economic and strategic interests, public health, safety, the environment and natural resources; (ii) delinks the revenue and regulatory functions of licensing; (iii) harmonizes licensing with other aspects of the start start-up process; (iv) repeals the Industrial Licensing Act; (v) removes the requirement for firms licensed under sector laws, to also have a general business license; and (vi) establishes a code of conduct on best practices to eliminate licensing bureaucracy.

Increasing Access to Land

Access to land, workspace, and productive resources is critical to unlocking the economic potential of women, but despite positive land reforms, land tenure in Tanzania continues to discriminate against women because of traditional practices and customary laws. This is particularly the case in relation to inheritance and in circumstances of the death of, or divorce from a spouse. Women are estimated to own about 19 percent of registered land, and their plots are less than half the size

Table 2. International Benchmarking: Company Formation

Country	Cost (% GNI per capita)	Duration (days)	No. of procedures
New Zealand	0.2	12	2
Canada	0.9	3	2
Australia	1.8	2	2
Kenya	46.3	54	13
Tanzania	91.6	30	13

Source: World Bank. 2006. Doing Business in 2007: How to Reform. Washington, DC.

of those of their male counterparts (0.21–0.30 ha compared to 0.61–0.70 ha; IFAD 2005; Bureau of Statistics 1994). Recommended reforms include the following:

- Strengthening enforcement of existing land laws and the dissemination of knowledge about women's property rights, why land is a valuable resource, and on other resources available to mortgage loans.
- Consideration should be given to amending s.60 Law of Marriage Act on the Mainland to provide that property acquired during the marriage in the name of either husband or wife belongs to both spouses, unless the contrary is established.
- Tanzania's (mainland) laws on inheritance should be reviewed and repealed, as appropriate, to create a uniform law of inheritance.

Improving Women's Access to Finance

Because women are not generally named—nor are their interests noted—on land titles, it is difficult for them to access formal sources of credit, which are mostly tied to the provision of titled land as collateral. Only about 5 percent of Tanzanian women are estimated to be currently banked (figure 3). The use of nonland assets as collateral is a problem, due to an outdated law and a poorly functioning system relating to the registration of personal property securities.

Asset leasing is a particularly important financial product for those who do not have land to use as collateral, who have no banking history, or who have limited start-up capital. However, the provision and use of leasing are constrained in Tanzania for numerous reasons relating to judicial

Figure 3. Banking Profile in Tanzania

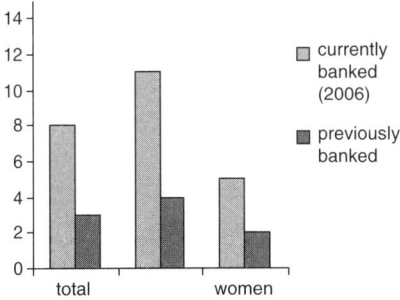

Source: FSDT (2007).

interpretation and enforcement of the law, unfavorable tax treatment, and lack of public awareness. Recommendations include the following:

- Encourage existing commercial banks to establish gender-sensitive programs or lines of credit for women entrepreneurs. Bankers should be trained to provide gender-sensitive customer care to female entrepreneurs.
- Consider reforming the law relating to secured transactions, using the UNCITRAL model, and instituting a computer-based system of registration.
- Introduce appropriate leasing legislation that clarifies the rights and responsibilities of the parties and provides simplified mechanisms for enforcing a lease agreement and repossessing leased assets.

Reforming Labor Laws

Despite high economic participation rates, women are mostly concentrated in casual, low-skilled, poorly remunerated, and irregular forms of informal sector employment. Although recent labor law reforms offer promising new protection for women in employment, they have the potential to end up hurting those they intend to help if employers find that compliance with them is too costly, or if they cannot be properly enforced. Recommendations include the following:

- Apply regulatory impact assessment analysis to all new proposed labor policies and laws to ensure that they are effective and affordable for employers, and that distributional impacts are fair and even.
- Track the impact of newly introduced labor laws.

Enhancing Access to Justice

Poor people in general and women in particular lack information about their rights and about access to mechanisms to enforce them. The Tanzania Women Lawyers Association explains that law enforcement institutions such as the police and the courts often reinforce male authority, and the fact that few women have business experience equal to that of men makes them vulnerable to unscrupulous business deals. In commercial instances, reliance on informal or traditional dispute resolution mechanisms can be problematic because of cultural prejudices and customary laws, yet access to higher courts is complicated and costly. Recommendations are as follows:

- Support reform of the Civil Procedure Code and introduce small claims divisions within magistrate's courts, which deal with commercial cases under a certain value and are presided over by specialized judges with training in commercial law.

- Establish and expand existing women's clinics (possibly annexed to the primary courts) through which women could receive ongoing education on commercial laws, legal rights, court procedures, and guidance on preparing claims and pleadings. Increase awareness among women entrepreneurs on magistrate issues.
- Prioritize the implementation of a sex-disaggregated baseline survey to identify challenges in the delivery of commercial justice.

Improving Access to International Trade

Trade plays an important role in Tanzania's development, and positive investment climate reforms, including trade facilitation policy reforms, have augmented Tanzania's export share and investment potential. Yet trade agreements, policies and mechanisms can have different impacts on men and women. Tanzania's Ministry of Industry, Trade and Marketing is very conscious of the gender dimensions of trade policy, having sent key staff to Geneva for training and ensuring gender focal points in all three departments. Women can also be disadvantaged when dealing with customs and are not well placed to protect their intellectual property rights. Recommendations include the following:

- Implement gender analysis in the formulation of trade and economic growth policies.
- Conduct workshops and provide practical training for women entrepreneurs on international buyer requirements and other relevant information, to facilitate their exports to international markets.
- Improve access by women to information about the rights and duties of exporters and importers, customs procedures, valuation processes for duty purposes, the limits of authority of customs officers, and appeals processes.
- Embark on a widespread information campaign to help entrepreneurs understand the importance of intellectual property protection and the applicable procedures.

This report is organized as follows. Chapter 1 examines the links among gender, economic growth, and poverty; chapters 2, 3, 4, and 5 focus on legal and administrative barriers that impede the ability of women to operate a business, as well as access to land and finance; chapter 6 examines the gender implications of labor laws; chapter 7 looks at the vital issue of women's access to commercial justice. Chapter 8 analyzes women's access to trade, and chapter 9 identifies entry points for reform.

Notes

1. World Economic Forum (2006). Interpreting these results requires caution since the index measures only gaps, not levels, and relies on labor force participation rates, which are problematic in Sub-Saharan Africa.
2. Replacing its *Women in Development Policy* of 1992.

Matrix of Recommendations

Gender and Economic Growth in Tanzania: Matrix of Recommendations

Issue	Recommendation	Impact/Timing	Responsibility
Starting and Closing a Business	*Starting a Business*		
Tanzania's formerly time-consuming and complex business registration, incorporation, and licensing practices had disproportionately adverse effects on women entrepreneurs, creating barriers to formalization and growth. Recent changes have substantially improved the situation, but the benefits have yet to be felt by many SMEs. Some new licenses are being introduced at the local level, and a complex sector licensing regime remains in place. Bureaucratic procedures, especially on issuing of business licenses at the municipal and local government level, still exist. Although the government recently introduced a new Companies' Act, company incorporation and compliance with the Act are still complex, time-consuming	Consider the introduction of best practice models for company formation and operation that provide simplified, low-cost procedures and reporting requirements applicable to small companies;	High/medium term	**TLS**/BEST/MoJCA
	Conduct targeted information campaigns for women that focus on the benefits of, and processes associated with, company incorporation.	Moderate/medium term	**TAMWA**/TCC/BRELA
	Design and implement a policy on sector licensing that (i) limits regulation strictly to areas where there is a clear necessity to preserve national security, key economic and strategic interests, public health, safety, the environment, and natural resources; (ii) delinks the revenue and regulatory functions of licensing (iii) harmonizes licensing with other aspects of the start-up process; (iv) repeals the Industrial Licensing Act; (v) removes the requirement for firms licensed under sector laws to also hold a general business license; and (vi) establishes a code of conduct on best practices to eliminate licensing bureaucracy.	High/medium term	**BEST**/MoTTM/ TWCC/sectoral ministries **BEST**/BRELA/ TWCC/Local government authorities
	Establish a business registry system that is accessible at the local level, and which features (i) links to other registries involved in business start-up; (ii) provision of information to businesses on	Moderate/medium term	**BEST**/BRELA/ MoTTM/MOJCA sectoral ministries

(continued)

Gender and Economic Growth in Tanzania: Matrix of Recommendations (continued)

Issue	Recommendation	Impact/Timing	Responsibility
processes, and continuing improvement is needed.	relevant fees, levies, regulations, compliance standards, and contact points in sectoral ministries; (iii) provision of relevant application forms; and (iv) provision of notice to the relevant district administration and sectoral agencies on the business. Establish time limits for the granting of administrative approvals, standardize and simplify forms, provide widespread information in Kiswahili on business entry procedures and any changes. Ensure all baseline and M&E data are sex disaggregated to better measure gender impacts.		
Access to Land and Site Development Access to land, workspace, and productive resources is critical to unlocking the economic potential of Tanzanian women, but land tenure in Tanzania discriminates against women because of the traditional practices and customary laws that govern it, particularly with regard to inheritance rights, and in situations involving divorce from, or death of, a spouse.	Strengthen enforcement of land laws and the dissemination of knowledge about women's property rights, information as to why land is a valuable resource, and on other resources available to mortgage loans. Disseminate training manuals aimed at magistrates and customary leaders, and informative leaflets aimed at the community, that record statute and case law establishing women's entitlement to property and support upon the death of and divorce from a spouse, to reduce cultural inhibitions and traditional attitudes preventing women from accessing justice. Centers should be established in rural areas where women entrepreneurs could access relevant information for their businesses. Support widespread dissemination of simplified versions of the land laws.	High/ immediate and ongoing High/ immediate	**TAWLA**/ MKURABITA, Ministries responsible for land in mainland and Zanzibar **TAWLA/TLS**/MoJ TWJA
	Property Rights During Marriage Consideration could be given to amending s.60 Law of Marriage Act (Mainland) to provide that property acquired during the marriage	High/ medium to	**TAWLA**/TWJA/ MoJCA/

in the name of either the husband or the wife, belongs to both spouses unless the contrary is established. This would conform to s.161 of the Land Act, 1999 and would prevent husbands from dealing separately with matrimonial property, but might also discourage women from acquiring separate property during the marriage. Views could be canvassed regarding this issue.	longer term	MCDGC
Property Laws on the Death of a Spouse Tanzania's (mainland) laws on inheritance should be reviewed and repealed as appropriate to create a uniform law of inheritance, and bring the law into line with the constitution, CEDAW, and CRC. Consideration could be given to the concept of giving a widow a life interest in the matrimonial home, protecting the ability of a widow to stay in the matrimonial home during her lifetime while allowing the land to revert to the husband's clan on her death.	High/ immediate	**TAWLA**/TLS/ TWJA/ MoJCA/ MCDGC
Property Rights on Divorce Review the requirement in Section 114 (2) Law of Marriage Act (Mainland), which obliges a court to have regard to the customs of the community to which the parties belong. The law could provide that a court should have regard to the customs of the community to which the parties belong, so long as they are not inconsistent with the constitution. In addition, instead of having regard to the extent of the contributions made by each party in money, property, or work toward acquiring matrimonial assets, the court could be required to have regard to extent of the contributions made by each party to the marriage (including acquisition of matrimonial assets), and to the care of the family.	High/ medium term	**MKURABITA**/ Ministries responsible for land in mainland and Zanzibar/ World Bank Competitiveness Project

(continued)

13

Gender and Economic Growth in Tanzania: Matrix of Recommendations *(continued)*

Issue	Recommendation	Impact/Timing	Responsibility
	Site Development Review town planning legislation to ensure provision of a compulsory requirement that serviced workspace for micro- and small-scale enterprises be earmarked and set aside in urban development plans. Consider facilitating the establishment of production clusters for women entrepreneurs, for example in basketry, pottery, and so forth.		
Access to Finance The practice of demanding titled land as collateral for loans is a particular problem for women, owing to their limited land ownership. An efficient, secure, and reliable system for registering nonland assets as collateral would encourage financiers to lend against nonland assets.	*Reforming the Chattels Transfer Act and Some Parts of the Companies Act* Consider reforming the law relating to secured transactions, using the UNCITRAL model, and instituting a computer-based system of registration. Widespread information dissemination on the law and procedures relating to secured transactions would need to accompany this reform.	High/ immediate	**BEST/** BRELA/TLS/ TAWLA/MoJ/ TCC
	Given the costly and time-consuming nature of establishing a new institution to lend to women, encourage existing commercial banks to establish gender sensitive programs, or lines of credit for women entrepreneurs. Bankers should be trained to have positive mindsets and provide gender-sensitive customer care to female entrepreneurs.	High/ immediate	**IFC/local** **commerical** **bank**
The provision and use of asset leasing are constrained because of problems associated with the judicial interpretation of rights and	*Access to Lease Finance* Enact appropriate enabling leasing legislation that clarifies the rights and responsibilities of the parties and provides simplified mechanisms for enforcing a lease agreement and repossessing leased assets.	High/ immediate	**BOT/MoF** **IFC leasing** project/BEST

obligations under lease contracts, enforcing lease contracts, and repossession of leased assets. Given women's difficulties in accessing traditional sources of lending, the importance of removing obstacles to the growth of the leasing industry in Tanzania cannot be understated.	Review the Hire Purchase Act to ensure that domestic consumer protection controls are not imposed on leasing transactions that involve capital equipment as opposed to personal property. Review the tax treatment of leasing to encourage new entrants to the sector. Review the VAT treatment of leasing so that the application of VAT does not operate to discourage the use and provision of leasing. Production of model agreement and explanatory handbook would be helpful in assisting lessors and lessees in framing and understanding their rights and obligations.	Moderate/ medium term	**BoT/IFC leasing project**/TRA
Dealing with Taxation Women, who tend to be less well educated than men and who are "time poor," find it difficult to comply with complex tax compliance procedures, and may be more subject to harassment and intimidation and demands for bribes.	Introduce special tax clinics for women to help them better understand the advantages of keeping records, the disadvantages of staying outside the VAT net, VAT and tax compliance issues, and the advantages of formalization. Collect gender disaggregated data on all taxes, and the annual TRA taxpayer perceptions survey should collect and analyze gender disaggregated data. TRA could support a study on tax constraints faced by women, including its relationship with women taxpayers, and support training for women to help them overcome constraints identified. It could also consider establishing a women's desk dedicated to the provision of advice and guidance to woman entrepreneurs.	High/ immediate	**TGNP/** TRA/TWCC
Local-Level Taxes At the local level, multiple and duplicative taxes (including fees and charges) make business entry difficult and expensive. Levies	*Local-Level Taxes* Continue reform and streamlining of the local government tax system, monitor revenue collection in relation to service delivery, offer incentives for the adoption of a customer service culture and	Moderate/ ongoing	**BEST/** LGRP/PMO-RALG/TPSF

(continued)

Gender and Economic Growth in Tanzania: Matrix of Recommendations *(continued)*

Issue	Recommendation	Impact/Timing	Responsibility
are perceived as exorbitant, often charged upfront, regardless of the size and type of business. Harsh and coercive enforcement practices are particularly problematic for women.	client charters within local governments, and encourage the introduction of penalties for use of unduly harsh and unlawful enforcement practices		
Tax Appeals—Up-front Deposit An up-front deposit of one-third of the disputed amount, or the amount of tax not in dispute, whichever is the greater, discourages tax appeals.	*Tax Appeals—Up-front Deposit* Consideration could be given to changing this provision so that payment is based on the taxpayer's calculation of what they owe, with heavy penalties if this leads to underpayment.	Moderate/ medium– longer term	**TRA**/BEST/ TPSF/CTI
Reliability of Infrastructure Lack of adequate infrastructure for water, energy, and transport imposes greater work burdens and lengthens the time it takes women to perform activities related to household survival, reducing the time for participating in other economic or income-generating activities as well as reducing agribusiness income opportunities for women.	Energy policy should focus on alternative energy sources to address the domestic energy needs of households, especially with regard to cooking fuels. Transport interventions should focus on improving women's access to transport services to reduce women's time burdens.	Moderate/ medium to longer term	**Millennium Challenge Corporation**/ Foundation for Civil Society/ Ministries of Energy and Transport
Access to Day Care Prescriptive and costly requirements and procedures in the Day Care Centers Act mean that professional day care is very	Reform the Day Day Care Centers Act on the mainland so that registration requirements are simple, practical, and affordable, to encourage more entrants to the sector and allow more women to take	High/ medium term	**TAWLA/MCDGC** in Mainland and Zanzibar

expensive, limited, and beyond the means of most working women.	advantage of the services offered by day care centers. Promulgate a low-compliance-cost Day Care Act for Zanzibar.		
Labor Laws A critical issue is to ensure that the right balance is struck between labor protection and job security, and flexibility for employers, especially in the context of Tanzania's relatively low labor productivity figures compared with its regional and international neighbors, and the importance of relative unit labor costs.	Raise awareness about rights and obligations under the laws through information campaigns, particularly on the radio; Regulatory impact assessment analysis should be applied to all proposed new labor policies and laws to ensure that they are effective and affordable to employers, and to ensure that distributional impacts are fair and even. Consider alternatives to regulation, as well as other regulatory options, before the proposed measures are introduced. Track the impact of newly introduced labor laws, and incorporate indicators in the BEST Programme's monitoring and evaluation framework that go beyond the current ease of hiring and firing, to encompass labor unrest, cost and coverage of workers' compensation, costs of complying with OSH, dispute resolution costs, maternity leave compliance rates, and formal labor force participation rates.	High/ immediate	**Ministries of Labor for Mainland and Zanzibar/** BEST/MPEE/LRCT
Access to Commercial Justice Tanzanian women are particularly disadvantaged when accessing justice because of their poverty, lack of awareness of their rights, discrimination by court officials based on traditional attitudes, and the high costs involved.	*Access to Commercial Justice* Prioritize the conduct of a gender-disaggregated baseline survey on the delivery of commercial justice in Tanzania to identify challenges in access to and dispensation of commercial justice. Capture statistics on the numbers of female and male plaintiffs coming before the courts, the subject area of the dispute, and in whose favor the judgment was made, to identify whether perceptions about unfair access to the courts and inequitable dispensation of justice are justified by evidence.	High/ immediate Moderate/ medium term	**BEST/MoJCA/** TGNP TWJA/ judiciary/

(continued)

Gender and Economic Growth in Tanzania: Matrix of Recommendations (continued)

Issue	Recommendation	Impact/Timing	Responsibility
	Support reform of the Civil Procedure Code, and introduce small claims divisions within Magistrates' Courts that deal with commercial cases under a certain value and are presided over by specialized judges with training in commercial law.	Moderate/ medium term	**BEST/ MoJCA**
	Establish and expand existing women's clinics (possibly annexed to the primary courts) through which women could receive ongoing education on commercial laws, legal rights, court procedures, and guidance on preparing claims and pleadings. Increase awareness among women entrepreneurs on magistrate issues.	High/ medium term	**TAWLA/** Judiciary/BEST
	Support the routine dissemination of up-to-date case law to judicial officers across the country. Ensure translations of decisions into Swahili; and establish information centers in courts for provision of information to the public on the law and legal rights.	High/ medium term	
Access to International Trade Women entrepreneurs lack information on international buyer requirements and on accessing the global marketplace, and often lack confidence to enter into international trade competitions, thereby limiting their ability to export.	*Access to International Trade* Conduct workshops and provide practical training for women entrepreneurs on international buyer requirements and other relevant information, to facilitate their exports to international markets.	High/ immediate	**IFC/MoTTM**
Export Processing Zones (EPZs) Promotion of export-oriented production in EPZs can provide unprecedented job	*EPZs* Conduct a survey on working conditions for women in EPZs; Women should be represented on the EPZ Council, on EPZ management	High/ medium term	**MoTTM/ZIPA** TNGP/NDC/

opportunities for women, but can also lead to women's being overrepresented in low-paid, low-skilled, export-oriented sectors where they face employment insecurity, unhealthy conditions, lack of protection, gender stereotypes and sexual harassment.	boards and on the business forums. A key focus of these forums must be ensuring that regulations, especially labor and health and safety regulations, are properly and fairly implemented;		
Dealing with Customs	*Dealing with Customs*		
Key concerns are the potential for abuse of wide discretionary powers, which women are less equipped to deal with than are their male counterparts. Women also lack clear information on rights and obligations, which makes them vulnerable to poor enforcement behavior and poor service attitudes by tax officials.	Specify in the Customs & Excise Management Act the limits of authority and responsibility of all officers in the customs process, and institute procedural guidelines that govern the handling and disposal of goods;	High/ medium term	**NDC/MCDGC/** TRA/industry associations
	Improve access by women to information about the rights and duties of exporters and importers, customs procedures, valuation processes for duty purposes, the limits of authority of customs officers, and appeals processes;	High/ short term	
	Mandate representation on the Customs and Excise stakeholders' forum from women in the trading community; consultations should be regularized, formalized, and focused on receiving input from the private sector on constraints and proposed actions.		
Enforcement of Intellectual Property (IP) Rights	*Enforcement of Intellectual Property Rights*		
Costly registration, the lack of information on accessing intellectual property right protection, and time-consuming procedures can discourage "time poor" women from protecting their innovations. Serious	Embark on a widespread information campaign to help entrepreneurs understand the importance of intellectual property protection and the applicable procedures;	High/ short term	**RULU Arts/** TWCC/COSOTA BRELA/MoTTM Reg of Trademarks (Z)
	Streamline and simplify registration procedures and ensure they are as low-cost as possible.		

(continued)

19

Gender and Economic Growth in Tanzania: Matrix of Recommendations *(continued)*

Issue	Recommendation	Impact/Timing	Responsibility
resource and human constraints within COSOTA prevent it from carrying out its mandate effectively.	Conduct needs assessment study of COSOTA to identify gaps in capacity and resources for carrying out its mandate. Support sustained lobbying of politicians and the Executive on the importance to Tanzania of building the COSOTA's labor and institutional capacity to the level that will enable it to become self-sustaining; Lobby for provision of funds to implement Hakigram project.		RULU Arts/ BEST AC/COSOTA
Trade Policy Development Inclusion of women in policy formulation and gender analysis in the formulation of trade and economic growth policies and programs would enable policy makers to mitigate adverse effects and develop compensatory measures of trade issues on women entrepreneurs.	*Trade Policy Development* Implementing gender analysis in the formulation of trade and economic growth policies and programs, and providing technical capacity building in gender analysis for public, private, and civil society representatives, will help ensure that the costs and benefits of trade reforms and agreements are spread evenly across society. To effectively disseminate the trade policy, a popular, reader-friendly version that includes interpretation of technical issues should be prepared.	High/ short term	**MoTTM**/TGNP
The Mining Subsector Women play a central role in small-scale mining operations, but their efforts are constrained by lack of finance for capital equipment, and by lack of capacity to conduct feasibility studies, construct business plans and financial forecasts, and understand tax and accounting requirements.	*The Mining Subsector* Consideration should be given to significantly extending the period of a small miner's prospecting license. TAWOMA suggests that government would signal its support for small-scale mining by announcing a national small-scale miners' day to raise the profile of the industry, enable miners to get together to trade skills, and help bring media and other attention to the exploitative conditions under which women miners are	Moderate/ medium term High/ immediate	**TAWOMA**/ Ministry of Energy **TAWOMA**/ Ministry of Energy

The prospecting license period under the Mining Act is too short. Rural women miners are subject to serious exploitation.	working. They would also like to see support for capacity building for women miners on issues such as mineral identification, for attending national and international exhibitions, market linkage facilitation through programs such as study tours to learn best practices from other countries, and encouragement of special financing programs to support small-scale miners.		
Strengthening of Women's Advocacy Although a variety of organizations implement gender advocacy, women's views and advocacy have not been well represented in ongoing business-related reform processes.	Provide training on media and advocacy skills, to enable women to make their case effectively to policy makers and bring about change, and provide financial and advisory support to increase women's capacity in advocacy.	High/ immediate	**IFC/BEST**

CHAPTER 1

Gender and Economic Growth in Tanzania

"How do we partner to build a better life for women? Empowering women by giving them financial independence should be the motto."

—Mary Nagu,
Minister of Justice and Constitutional Affairs[1]

This chapter addresses gender roles in the Tanzanian economy and their implications for growth, productivity, and welfare. This is an important building block for understanding the relevance of gender as an economic issue in Tanzania, and for identifying key actions to tap the full productive potential of both males and females in the Tanzanian economy.

Tanzania completed its National Strategy for Growth and Reduction of Poverty (NSGRP, or MKUKUTA in Kiswahili) in June 2005. The MKUKUTA calls for annual GDP growth of 6–8 percent to 2009–2010. Although gender is identified as a cross-cutting issue, specific measures to address gender-based obstacles to growth and poverty reduction are not identified. This assessment will, therefore, help fill an important gap in specifying gender-inclusive measures to facilitate the MKUKUTA's growth and poverty reduction objectives.

Women and Men in the Tanzanian Economy

Whereas both men and women play substantial roles in Tanzania's economy, women are more active in agriculture than men, specifically in food crop production (primarily maize) and in the processing of agricultural products. Of 17.8 million economically active people, 16.9 million are considered employed, and of these, women constitute 50.6 percent (For data from Zanzibar, see box 1.1).[2] The unemployment rate is estimated at 5.4 percent of economically active people and, by this definition, 57.5 percent of unemployed are women. The overall labor force participation rate of women is—at 80.7 percent—slightly higher than that of men (79.6 percent).[3] Since Tanzania is a largely agriculture-dominated economy, the sector absorbs 82 percent of the labor force—either as self-employed, unpaid family workers, or those working for wages (URT 2002a). By these measures, the concentration of the female labor force in agriculture (84.2 percent) is slightly higher than that of men (80.2 percent) (table 1.2).

The distribution of men and women across the sectors is uneven: Women are slightly in the majority in agriculture (52 percent versus 48 percent) and in trade (55 percent versus 45 percent), whereas men dominate in manufacturing, construction, transport, and finance. The distribution of economic activity by type of employment is uneven too,

Box 1.1

Labor in Zanzibar

Data for Zanzibar in 1996 indicate a total labor force of 393,150 (aged 15–65 years), of which 53 percent were men. Formal employment absorbed only 8 percent of the labor force, of which 30 percent were women. Female employment is concentrated in agriculture and self-employment, and in informal sector or home-based production more than in formal employment. This is partly due to inadequate education and qualifications for women, preventing them from competing for formal sector jobs and partly to the need to create an enabling environment to stimulate society as a whole. Women are also subject to cultural perspectives on the kinds of jobs "acceptable" for females. For example, the majority of female workers in the tourism industry are from the mainland, since Zanzibari women are reported to believe such work is inappropriate for them.

Source: African Development Bank (2005).

Table 1.1. Economically Active Population, by Sex, 2000–01

	Economically active	Employed	Unemployed
Male	8,739,708	8,351,291	388,417
Female	9,087,869	8,563,514	524,355
Total	17,827,577	16,914,805	912,772
In percent			
Male	49.02	49.37	42.55
Female	50.98	50.63	57.45

Source: United Republic of Tanzania (2002a).

showing important gender differences. Only 4.0 percent of women are in paid jobs, in either the formal or informal sector, compared with 9.8 percent of men (table 1.3).

Gender disparities are also evident in formal sector employment, where men account for 71 percent of workers. According to data from the Employment and Earnings Survey of 2001, the ratio of women to men in formal sector employment is 0.41 (URT 2004). This is high compared with other SSA countries (0.34 in 2000), but is still significantly below East Asia (0.66) for the same period (Klasen and Lamanna 2003). The private sector exhibits a somewhat smaller ratio of women to men, at 0.39, whereas the ratio is 0.48 in the public sector. Men tend to be much better represented among regular waged employees than women. Table 1.4 shows that, in the manufacturing sector where the waged employment rate is highest, only 18.6 percent of employees are women.

According to the Country Economic Memorandum (World Bank 2007), more than 80 percent of Tanzania's poor derive their livelihoods from agriculture. Between 1991 and 2000, the agriculture sector grew by an average of 3.5 percent, which suggests per capita growth of less than 1 percent. The increase in per capita expenditure by farm households was equally modest, at 7.3 percent over the period 1991–1992 to 2000–2001. Nevertheless, this explains more than half of the total decline in poverty observed during that period. Between 2000 and 2005, growth in the agriculture sector accelerated to an average of 4.8 percent annually, which is likely to have generated a further drop in rural poverty. Given Tanzania's agricultural potential, there is significant scope for reducing poverty by fostering growth in this sector, thereby increasing farming incomes.

The Participatory Poverty Assessment (PPA) highlighted not only the importance of agriculture in poverty reduction, but also its critical gender dimensions. As reported in the PPA: "a remarkable 47 percent of all responses about the causes of poverty were related to being able to farm

Table 1.2. Distribution of Currently Employed Persons, by Sex and Sector, 2000–01

Sex	Agriculture, forestry, fishing	Mining and quarrying	Manufactures	Electricity and gas	Construction	Trade	Transport	Finance	Personal services	Total
Male	6,698,817	15,452	161,699	13,464	147,494	565,495	103,929	22,162	622,779	8,351,291
Female	7,191,237	13,771	83,750	1,233	4,196	697,473	7,643	4,339	559,872	8,563,514
Total	13,890,054	29,223	245,449	14,697	151,690	1,262,968	111,572	26,501	1,182,651	16,914,805
In percent (by column)										
Male	48.2%	52.9%	65.9%	91.6%	97.2%	44.8%	93.1%	83.6%	52.7%	49.4%
Female	51.8%	47.1%	34.1%	8.4%	2.8%	55.2%	6.9%	16.4%	47.3%	50.6%
Total	100.0%	100.0%	100.0%	100.0%	100.0%	100.0%	100.0%	100.0%	100.0%	100.0%
In percent (by row)										
Male	80.2%	0.2%	1.9%	0.2%	1.8%	6.8%	1.2%	0.3%	7.5%	100.0%
Female	84.0%	0.2%	1.0%	0.0%	0.0%	8.1%	0.1%	0.1%	6.5%	100.0%
Total	82.1%	0.2%	1.5%	0.1%	0.9%	7.5%	0.7%	0.2%	7.0%	100.0%

Source: United Republic of Tanzania (2002a).

Table 1.3. Percentage of Currently Employed Persons, by Employment Status

Employment status	Current employment %			Female (Male = 100)
	Male	Female	Total	
Paid employment	9.8	4.0	6.9	40.8
Self-employment	8.9	7.8	8.3	87.6
Unpaid helper	3.0	4.6	3.8	153.3
Agriculture (own farm/shamba)	78.2	83.6	81.0	109.6
Total	**100**	**100**	**100**	

Source: Data from United Republic of Tanzania (2002a), and staff calculations.

Table 1.4. Wage Employment, by Sex in Selected Sectors, 2001

Sector	Number			Share (%)		
	Male	Female	Total	Male	Female	Total
Agriculture	34,472	11,456	45,928	75.06	24.94	100
Manufacturing	65,411	14,900	80,311	81.45	18.55	100
Commerce	54,659	21,577	76,236	71.70	28.30	100
Transport and communication	46,677	9,651	56,328	82.87	17.13	100

Source: URT (2004). The data refer to persons who are regularly employed in enterprises with at least five employees. The table includes only workers aged 16 or older.

Table 1.5. Division of Labor in Agriculture

Task	%	
	F	M
General Crop Production	56	44
Food Crop Production	75	25
Land Tilling	56	44
Sowing	74	26
Weeding	70	30
Harvesting	71	29
Marketing	73	27

Source: National Sample Census of Agriculture, 1996, in Keller (1999).

productively" (Narayan 1997). Whereas men focused on the processes of farming, women focused on the consequences of poor farming—low yields, food shortage, high prices, lack of cash, migration, and hunger. Census data on men's and women's roles in agriculture show the dominant role of women in the sector, including in marketing (table 1.5).

The ILFS data indicate that almost all rural households (98 percent) are involved in agriculture. The structure of the rural labor market is summarized in table 1.6 below.

Table 1.6. Distribution of Currently Employed Persons in the Rural Labor Force, by Sex and Status

| | By Sex | | | | | |
| | Male | | Female | | Total | |
Area/employment status	Number	%	Number	%	Number	%
Paid employee	362,528	2.6	101,792	0.7	464,320	3.3
Self-employed without employee	280,442	2.0	164,060	1.2	444,502	3.2
Unpaid family helper (nonagriculture)	186,604	1.3	282,835	2.0	469,439	3.4
Agriculture (own farm/shamba)	6,055,955	43.3	6,562,260	46.9	12,618,215	90.2
Total	6,885,529	49.2	7,110,946	50.8	13,996,476	100.0

Source: NBS/URT 2002. *Integrated Labour Force Survey Report.*

In its *Small and Medium Enterprise Development Policy 2000*, the government acknowledges both the importance of the small and medium enterprise (SME) sector to growth and the role of women in that sector. In terms of incomes, SME sector entrepreneurs generated 2.5–10 times the minimum income of public sector employees (1991 Informal Sector Survey, cited by IFAD 2005). The International Labour Organization (2003) estimates that the number of Tanzanian women entrepreneurs ranges from 730,000 to 1.2 million. They are particularly found in the MSME sector, where they are estimated to make up 43 percent of the total (IFAD 2005).

Nonmarket Work and Time Use

In addition to their prominence in agriculture, women bear the brunt of domestic tasks that are often arduous, time-intensive, and energy-consuming. These include processing food crops, providing water and firewood, and caring for the elderly and the sick. This last task has assumed particular importance since the HIV/AIDS pandemic in Tanzania. The time and effort required for these duties, in the almost total absence of even rudimentary domestic technology, is very high. Yet this productive work is largely invisible and, in practice, not included in the System of National Accounts (SNA).[4]

Village transport surveys in Tanzania show that women spend nearly three times as much time in transport activities—including economic and domestic activities—compared with men, and they transport about four times as much in volume. Nearly half of the total time spent on transport tasks in villages in the Makete Region is spent on activities related to domestic tasks—fuel and water fetching and traveling to the grinding mill. Household chores are still a predominantly female task, and are a determining factor in how women use their time. Key tasks in the household economy are supplying energy through firewood collection,[5] and fetching water. By far the greater share of this is done by women, corresponding to nearly two hours each day (figure 1.1).[6] Women's transport needs are typically more complex than those of men, since they are engaged in domestic transport tasks, in transport associated with accessing social and economic services, and in economic activities that require transport of goods to market; adequately responding to these needs could increase women's contribution to economic productivity and qualitatively improve household welfare. Women's access to transport also determines their utilization of existing health and other services, and particularly affects the ability of girl children to attend school.

Since many factors add to the time burden of women, there are also many options to reduce that burden. For example, improving accessibility of water or investing in alternative energies has the potential to reduce substantially women's time constraint. Studies in Tanzania address the key dynamics at work and their implications for women's involvement in business activities (box 1.2).

Figure 1.1. Tanzania Transport Tasks

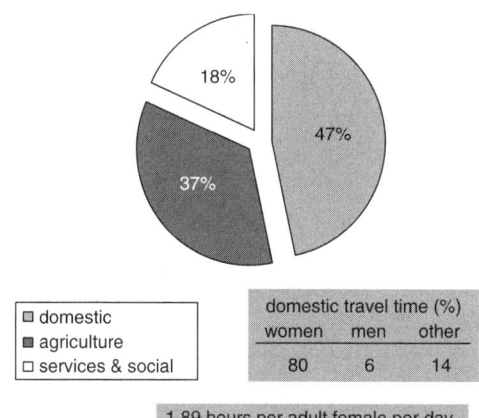

Source: Christina Malmberg-Calvo 1994, *Women in Rural Transport.* SSTP Working Paper No. 11. World Bank and ECA.

Box 1.2

Household Tasks, Time Use, and Entrepreneurship in Tanzania

Women play an important role in generating nonfarm income. However, time spent on household chores, such as fetching water or collecting firewood, proves to be a significant constraint on their participation in the off-farm labor market. Mduma uses HBS 2000–01 data on household access to piped water and the share of fuelwood in meeting energy needs as proxies for the time burden of women. In an analysis of female labor market participation, these factors prove to be negatively correlated to the probability of women engaging in off-farm employment. Seebens (2006) employs data on time spent fetching water and collecting firewood from the Kagera DHS to analyze the impact of time constraints on female off-farm employment. The results suggest a negative relationship between time taken up by these chores and the probability of starting an off-farm business. If the 10 hours a week now spent on these tasks were reduced by one hour, the probability of women engaging in off-farm business would increase by 7 percent. These results suggest that, alongside efforts to improve the business environment for women, investments in time-saving infrastructure such as piped water and modern or more accessible household energy have the potential to increase women's capacity to participate in off-farm income-generating activities. Investigating the impact of the availability of cheap energy on household labor, Rutamu (1999) finds that since the introduction of the biodigesters in Tanga, Muheza, and Usambara, households were able to reduce their daily labor burden by five hours. Women benefited most from this improvement, since the daily need to spend four hours collecting firewood was reduced to half an hour.

Sources: Mduma (2005); Rutamu (1999); Seebens (2006).

Men and Women Differ in Access to and Control of Productive Resources

Gender differences persist across many spheres in Tanzania, including in education, health, legal status, cultural perceptions, and in the economic arena. Most of these disparities have implications for the country's growth potential—agriculture, the mainstay of the economy, is likely to remain below its productivity frontier because of women's unequal access to land

and other productive resources. This section focuses on two key discrepancies affecting women's economic capacity: earnings and education.

Gender Disparities Exist With Respect to Earnings

The ILFS 2000–01 data show that in most paid labor occupations, men have substantially higher earnings compared to women. In manufacturing, the mean monthly income paid to women is T Sh 42,413, which is almost 3.5 times less than the average income earned by men (table 1.7). It is important to examine why such gaps persist, and their nature in different sectors. Along with analysis of gender-based differences in productivity, this would provide a foundation for addressing the extent to which low wages for women, together with their current low participation rates in the manufacturing sector, constitute a competitive advantage and opportunity for expansion of the export-oriented manufacturing sector. Entrepreneurs may take advantage of the fact that women with the same level of education as men command lower wages and are therefore more cost-effective; a phenomenon that has been a driving force behind the high economic growth rates in East and Southeast Asia (Seguino 2000). Nonetheless, it is important to take into account productivity differences, which may not be captured adequately in education data, and for Tanzania to examine the implications of these differences for competitiveness more carefully.

Female employment also has implications for the welfare and education of children, and for fertility (box 1.3). As incomes are often not pooled within households, and women are responsible for purchasing food and household goods, any increase in income earned by women leads to higher household expenditure on food and education. This relationship has been empirically demonstrated by Thomas (1990) and by Haddad and Hoddinott (1994), among others. In Tanzania, women's employment has also been found to reduce child labor (ILO 2001), as the income earned by women offsets the small amounts of supplemental income generated by children.

Gender Inequality Exists in Education

Tanzanian girls have clearly benefited from the legacy of Julius Nyerere, under whose rule universal education was promoted. In 2004, girls' gross primary school enrollment achieved a rate of 98.85 percent, whereas the gross primary school enrollment of boys sat at 102.84 percent, or a ratio of 0.96.

With respect to gross secondary school enrollment, progress in reducing gender disparities has been much slower. During the period 1970–1985,

Table 1.7. Mean Monthly Income of Paid Employees, by Sex and Sector, 2000–01

Sex	Agriculture, forestry, fishing	Mining and quarrying	Manufactures	Electricity and gas	Construction	Trade	Transport	Finance	Personal services
Male	16,318	78,800	122,435	89,848	49,885	37,556	82,280	144,253	69,440
Female	11,193	27,500	42,413	46,122	44,473	23,422	145,972	135,863	49,949
Female (Male = 100)									
	68.6	34.9	34.6	51.3	89.2	62.4	177.4	94.2	71.9

Source: United Republic of Tanzania (2002a).

Box 1.3

Population Growth in Tanzania

A key challenge for Tanzania will be to address demographic trends. Tanzania is one of the 35 countries in the world where the total fertility rate (TFR) is still higher than five children per woman. With a demographic growth rate currently estimated at 2.6 percent per year, the Tanzanian population of 38 million (2004 estimate) is expected to double in about 27 years. United Nations projections estimate that the country's population will reach 67 million by 2050, assuming very rapid fertility decline. In fact, it seems possible that fertility has not declined in Tanzania during the past 10 years—after an initial, although small—drop in the mid-1990s. This could mean that the fertility transition could take longer than currently projected. Rapid population growth presents a major and pressing challenge for the country, with far-reaching implications for human capital development, employment creation, and the environment, as well as for public services and resource mobilization.

the female-to-male enrollment ratio improved by 17 percentage points (from 0.40 to 0.57) and stood at 0.81 in 2000. Given that total secondary school enrollment is still very low, amounting to only 5.8 percent of the school-age population, the impact of current gender disparities in secondary education on future economic growth is likely to be low. The more important question is how to increase secondary enrollment for both boys and girls simultaneously. The government has adopted gender equity as a target for improving secondary schooling in its Secondary Education Master Plan (Mbelle and Katabaro 2003).

The female-to-male enrollment ratio in tertiary education stands at 0.31. Young women tend to be enrolled in nonengineering-related studies such as education, health science, or commerce. Female enrollment at the Sokoine University of Agriculture was 27.6 percent in 2001 (SUA 2007), a matter of some concern since—as indicated above—women constitute more than half the country's agricultural workforce.

Based on estimates of the average years of schooling, Tanzania's education outcomes are fairly poor (Barro and Lee 2000). The average has fallen somewhat from 2.82 years in 1970 to 2.71 in 2000, as shown in Table 1.8—a decline of nearly 4 percent. During this same period, the female-to-male ratio in average years of schooling has improved from

Table 1.8. Net School Enrollment Ratios and Average Years of Schooling, by Gender

Year	Prim. net enrollment (%)			Sec. net enrollment (%)			Average years of schooling		
	Total	Female	Male	Total	Female	Male	Total	Female	Male
1970	33.47	26.31	40.69	2.67	1.53	3.82	2.82	2.22	3.45
1975	52.64	43.79	61.65	3.15	1.96	4.36	2.62	2.03	3.24
1980	92.51	85.85	99.37	3.30	2.32	4.30	2.68	1.97	3.43
1985	75.11	74.05	76.20	3.27	2.37	4.18	2.87	2.16	3.63
1990	69.72	69.08	70.35	4.95	4.09	5.83	2.79	2.21	3.39
1995	66.81	66.10	67.51	5.44	4.90	5.99	2.68	2.23	3.16
2000	64.05	64.12	63.98	5.81	5.22	6.41	2.71	2.33	3.09

Source: World Bank (2004e), and Barro and Lee (2000).

0.64 to 0.75, reflecting a closing of the gender gap in education. This is the result of a 10 percent decline in average years of schooling for males, only partially offset by a 5 percent improvement for females.

Gender and Growth—Macro- and Microperspectives

Recent analysis of gender and growth has established a potential relationship between gender disparities and economic advance. Gender disparities, it is argued, hinder the development of equal opportunities and free markets, to the detriment of women, their families, and society as a whole. Despite progress in many areas, Tanzania is no exception. Inequalities in the formal labor market and at the higher levels of the education system, as shown above, have economic and social costs that may slow future growth.

There is a growing body of literature showing that gender differences in education, employment, access to assets, and time burdens have significant adverse impacts on an economy. Economic theory suggests that growth depends on the accumulation of economic assets (including human capital), and the returns on these assets. These, in turn, depend on technological progress, the efficiency with which assets are used, and the institutional context.

Gender issues will naturally come into play in the way all of these factors influence growth. With respect to access to education, there may be a selection-distortion effect in gender inequality, where less able boys may be educated instead of more able girls, thereby losing out on the potential human capital level in the economy. There are also indirect positive benefits for fertility and child mortality associated with female education. Better-educated women have been found to have fewer children and child mortality is also lower. This, in turn, lowers dependency ratios and facilitates participation in the workforce.

Beyond education, gender inequalities in employment reduce the skill pool available to employers, implying higher labor costs and lower economic competitiveness. In addition, inequalities in access to productive inputs distort economic incentives, thereby lowering productivity and output.

As has been shown above, women are more "time poor" than men, given their disproportionate responsibilities for household tasks. These time constraints reduce the ability of women to engage in market work, while their total labor effort is not fully captured or valued in national accounts.

Empirically, there is a body of international evidence supporting these theoretical linkages. Empirical studies on the relationship between gender disparities and economic growth have shown that this link is multifaceted, with direct and indirect implications. Essentially, the findings focus on three different issues: (i) the impact of limiting women's education and (formal) labor market participation; (ii) women's limited access to economically productive resources; and (iii) unequal remuneration for labor between men and women. Although these issues in part relate to conventional determinants of economic growth such as the investment rate and stocks of human capital, the analysis of the linkage between gender and growth need not be restricted to these aggregate variables. Women may face additional constraints, such as restricted access to credit, which keep them from investing in productivity-improving technologies.

So, gender disparities in access to education have been shown to have a significant adverse impact on economic growth rates (Dollar and Gatti 1999; Forbes 2000; Knowles et al. 2002; Klasen 2002; Yamarik and Ghosh 2003; Kalaitzidakis et al. 2001). Based on these empirical estimates, it is possible to determine an order of magnitude for possible growth effects in countries with gender inequalities in this area. For secondary education, using data for more than 100 countries, Dollar and Gatti (1999) estimate that an increase in one percentage point in the share of adult women with secondary education increases per capita income growth by 0.3 percentage points, on average (table 1.9). A background paper prepared for the Tanzania CEM (Utz 2005) estimated that an increase of 1.2 years in the average time spent at school leads to a one percentage point increase in growth. Using this hypothesis, the growth arising from equalizing female and male average years at school can be calculated—it would lead to an increase in growth of 0.63 percentage points.[7] These estimates are not disaggregated by sex, but, in view of the low levels of secondary enrollments in Tanzania, they point to a significant potential contribution to future growth from increasing both male and female secondary enrollments.

Table 1.9. Estimates of the Impact on GDP Growth of Bringing Female Secondary Schooling, and Female Total Years of Schooling to the Same Level as that of Males (%)

Equalization of the female to male ratio of	Yamarik and Ghosh	Dollar and Gatti	Klasen and Lamanna	CEM/ easterly
Secondary school enrollment		0.36		
Average years of schooling	0.15 to 0.53		0.17	0.63

Source: Authors.

Therefore, applying such international estimates to Tanzania would imply the following:

- An increase in per capita GDP growth of 0.36 percentage points if female secondary education enrollment were brought up to the level of male secondary enrollment.
- An increase in overall GDP growth of 0.15 to 0.63 percentage points if Tanzania brought total female years of schooling up to the same level as that of males, assuming no significant productivity differentials.

The calculations given in table 1.9 reinforce the importance for Tanzania of increasing total school enrollments without neglecting female schooling. And despite the many international studies concerned with the impact of gender disparity on growth, there appears to be only sporadic microlevel analysis of the costs incurred by gender inequality on economic growth in Tanzania (see box 1.4 for one example).[8]

Box 1.4

The Cost of Different Gender Roles in Agriculture—A Tanzania Case Study

A case study of banana and coffee growers in the Kagera region used a linear programming model to examine the implications of changes in the gender division of labor on productivity and output. Women are involved in almost all activities on the farm, including housework (in which the men hardly participate). Even in traditional male activities such as cash crop farming, women were found to make significant labor contributions. Surveys in the region established that women provided 52 percent of the labor for economic activity, compared with 42 percent for men. Men were estimated to have 4.5 hours of leisure time per day, compared with 2 hours per day for women. From these figures, scenarios comparing the traditional division of labor with partially and fully liberalized divisions of labor were developed. The results indicated that existing gender roles here are economically inefficient. If traditional gender roles in the farming system were to be abandoned, farm cash incomes could increase by up to 10 percent, while the productivity of labor and capital would improve by 15 and 44 percent respectively.

Source: Tibaijuka (1994).

It is important to interpret these figures with caution. They are useful in identifying orders of magnitude of possible effects, and are not intended to provide precise estimates or to imply causality. Such results are nonetheless fairly striking. Although not seeking to be definitive, they do suggest that gender inequality is a factor hampering economic growth, and that there is missed potential for accelerating growth through tackling gender-based obstacles.[9]

If Tanzania were to undertake a systematic effort to achieve gender parity in education and employment opportunities, and thereby to tap the economic potential of its women, it could make important strides in expanding economic growth. Our conservative estimates suggest that if the country were simply to bring female secondary schooling, and female total years of schooling to the same level as for males, that alone could produce up to an additional percentage point of growth. This would, in turn, make a valuable contribution to achieving or even exceeding the growth targets of the MKUKUTA. Given the small percentage of economic activity in the formal sector, encouraging enterpreneurship by promoting an efficient enabling environment for business is an important strategy for economic growth.

Notes

1. Speech at the World Bank/IFC organized workshop on the draft findings of the Tanzania Gender and Growth Assessment, February 26, 2007, Dar es Salaam, Tanzania.
2. For more information on how economic activity and employment are defined here, see appendix 1.
3. The World Economic Forum, in its 2006 Gender Gap Report (WEF 2006), ranks Tanzania number 1 among 115 countries in economic participation and opportunity. However, caution is required in interpreting this ranking, as the index does not take account of the different economic opportunities accessible to men and women. It only measures gaps and not levels, and relies on labor force participation rates that are problematic in SSA. For more on this, see the appendix.
4. The gender dimensions of time poverty are addressed further in Blackden and Wodon (2006).
5. In 2003, 92 percent of total energy consumption was from "traditional" sources (World Bank 2006d).
6. For data on gender and transport tasks in Tanzania, see Malmberg-Calvo (1994) and Barwell (1996).

7. The data in table 1.9 show that the gender gap in average years of schooling in 2000 is 0.76 years (3.09 male years of schooling, less 2.33 female years of schooling). If an increase of 1.2 years of schooling on average translates into one percentage point of higher growth, an increase of 0.76 years of female schooling would translate into a 0.63 percentage point increase in growth, assuming no gender-based differences in the contribution of years of schooling to growth.

8. See Udry (1996) for further results on the productivity losses of agricultural production owing to inefficient allocation of inputs between men and women in Burkina Faso. Smith and Chavas (1999) and von Braun and Webb (1989) demonstrate that the adoption of new technologies failed because women had to work on the husbands' fields without receiving compensation for their forgone personal income.

9. This point is made forcefully in World Bank (2000).

CHAPTER 2

Starting and Closing a Business

"To get licenses we did face problems. It took us a long time. It's not clear who has the mandate to give out the licenses."

—Victoria Kisyombe, Sero Lease and Finance Ltd.
Voices of Women Entrepreneurs in Tanzania

Although Tanzania has made commendable progress in reducing the cost of starting a business, business entry remains a challenge. Starting a business in Tanzania is still more costly than in Kenya at 46.3 percent and Uganda at 114 percent of income per capita, respectively (World Bank 2006a). Findings of the MKURABITA diagnostic study show that approximately 98 percent of all businesses operate extralegally because of the obstructive regulatory and administrative obstacles to registering, incorporating, and conducting their business activities (figure 2.1). The government has recognized that simplifying business entry procedures would encourage more Tanzanian entrepreneurs to join the formal economy. Given that women have many more competing demands on their time than men because of domestic and family care responsibilities, reducing the time it takes to comply with the bureaucratic hurdles of entering into business is likely to have a disproportionately positive impact on them.

Figure 2.1. Percentages of Businesses Operating and Properties Held Extralegally in Tanzania

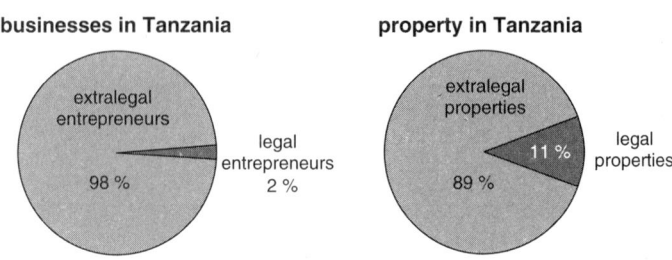

Source: Institute for Liberty and Democracy (2005).

Across countries, cumbersome entry procedures are associated with more corruption (World Bank 2006a). Each procedure is a point of contact—an opportunity to extract a bribe. Empirical analysis shows that burdensome entry regulations hold back private investment, push more people into the informal economy, increase consumer prices, and fuel corruption.

In Tanzania, there are three areas of law that provide the framework for business entry: companies legislation, business names registration, and business licensing legislation. While the government is committed to addressing these time-consuming, bureaucratic hurdles characterize each of these processes. According to the *Doing Business* data, it takes 35 days to fulfill all legal requirements for starting a business in Tanzania, at a cost of 91.6 income per capita. This is less time than neighbouring Kenya at 54 days, but the per capita cost is higher as shown in table 2.1 below. In Zanzibar, laws relating to business entry are dispersed throughout 63 decrees and statutes, which makes it difficult and costly for firms to get the information they require about how to comply.

Laws regulating business procedures are mostly available only in English, are subject to frequent amendments, and are not easy to obtain. Entry procedures are centralized in Dar es Salaam and Stone Town. This increases the costs and duration of the process, especially for those who have to travel in from rural areas.

The Costs of Starting a Business

Recognizing the cost to the economy of a complicated and costly business start-up regime, the Government of Tanzania recently embarked on a comprehensive reform program, which includes registration and licensing reforms, and the introduction of the Business Activities Registration Act of 2007 and a new Companies Act. The purpose of these reforms was to simplify and streamline business entry and formalization to increase competitiveness, but concerns remain about whether these objectives have been entirely fulfilled. The following sections explore these issues and the potential implications for women.

Company Formation Is Time-Consuming and Costly

"For all intents and purposes, our new Companies Act is the old one made more complicated!" according to Charles Rwechungura, at the time president of the Tanganyika Law Society.[1] Tanzania's new Companies Act introduced a number of detailed changes to the regulation of companies, but is largely a consolidation and clarification of Tanzanian company law, rather than fundamental reform, and remains based on U.K. law.[2] Unfortunately, U.K. company law is recognized by practitioners and academics as being highly problematic, because it focuses on the regulation of large, public companies, rather than companies that are small and privately owned, and because it is an uneasy amalgam of English common law and European law principles that have been incorporated into the act through European Union directives. As such, it seems to be an unsuitable model for Tanzania (Law & Development Partnership 2006).

The result of the reform is that complex and time-consuming requirements for company incorporation are perpetuated—costs that firms have an incentive to evade through informality (table 2.1). This incentive is even stronger for women entrepreneurs, who tend to be more time- and cash-constrained than their male counterparts.

Company law reforms undertaken in Australia, Canada, and New Zealand, the countries that have the fastest and least costly incorporation procedures in the world, may hold some lessons for Tanzania. Rather than

Table 2.1. International Benchmarking: Company Formation

Country	Cost (% GNI per capita)	Duration (days)	No. of procedures
New Zealand	0.2	12	2
Canada	0.9	3	2
Australia	1.8	2	2
Kenya	46.3	54	13
Tanzania	91.6	30	13

Source: World Bank (2006a).

Box 2.1

Key Company Law Reforms in Australia, Canada, and New Zealand

- Replacing the need for a Memorandum of Articles and Memorandum of Association with one simple registration form, which does away with the need to use lawyers
- Simplifying company law concepts, in particular nominal capital. This stream-lines company formation and makes running a company easier
- Simplifying registration procedures and providing for online registration with one registration fee

following the U.K. model for company law reform, these countries have undertaken a fundamental simplification of their company law (box 2.1). These reforms, which were initiated by the need to compete in a global economy and attract investment, have had a dramatic impact on the time and cost of company registration. Although the new Tanzania act has just been introduced, the benefits of further reform, particularly for female-headed businesses that struggle with greater time and resource constraints than their male counterparts, could be considerable. The World Bank's Doing Business in 2006 provides examples of increased business formation following reform: in Serbia, nearly 1,500 more firms registered in the first half of 2005 relative to the previous year—a 42 percent jump—and in Vietnam, Romania, and Belgium, new entries following reform, jumped by 28, 22, and 16 percent respectively.

Business Name Registration Imposes a Significant Burden

With the introduction of the Business Activities Registration Act, there will be a universal registration regime for businesses in Tanzania, and there should soon be a comprehensive national database of operating firms. However, the requirement to register under the Business Names (Registration) Act (Cap 213), for firms that wish to trade under a business name that is different from that of the founder, remains.

Findings from a recent survey of businesses show that registration under the Business Names (Registration) Act, which is meant to prevent firms from trading under the same name as another firm, imposes a significant

Figure 2.2. Registration Costs Have a Relatively Larger Impact on Micro-Businesses

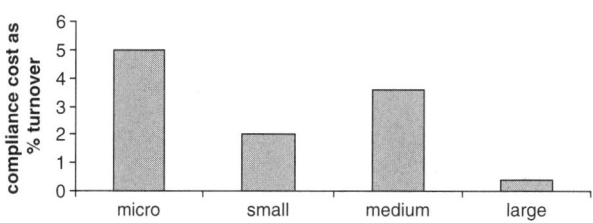

Source: Law & Development Partnership (2006).

burden on entrepreneurs (about 5 percent of turnover for microenterprises), as shown in figure 2.2 (Law & Development Partnership 2006). A less burdensome solution might be to require firms that consider it commercially worthwhile to protect their business name to voluntarily register the name as a trademark.

Licensing a Business Remains Problematic

All businesses must obtain clearances related to health, land or workspace, and tax (TIN, VAT and PAYE), register workers for social security purposes under the National Social Security Fund Act, and obtain insurance under the Workmen's Compensation Act. Once these clearances have been obtained, an entrepreneur must try to navigate the sectoral business licensing system (54 major types of business activities require sector specific licenses), which numerous studies note as being highly problematic.[3] With a few exceptions, business licensing is mandatory for all firms in Zanzibar under Trade Licensing Act No. 3 of 1983. The MKURABITA Diagnostic reports that "the current business licensing system generated the most complicated and burdensome part of gaining legal access to business both in Mainland and in Zanzibar. The system is complex, lacks inter-agency coordination, and has no established standards for the different requirements and inspections that arise during the paperwork process" (Institute for Liberty and Democracy 2005).

A large number of preconditions attach to sector-related licenses and the time to get the approvals encourages firms to shortcut the system through bribes, or evade compliance through informality. Although the delays and costs of registering a business and obtaining the relevant approvals are a burden for all businesses, the evidence is that the buren is worse for firms headed by women. This is because they are (i) more likely to suffer from physical harassment from regulatory officials, (ii) have less sophisticated networks for obtaining permits and licenses than their male counterparts, and (iii) have less access to information about permits and licenses than their male counterparts (Law & Development Partnership 2006).

In addition, given that women have far greater family and domestic responsibilities than men, and therefore less time to devote to business matters, it is likely that they will perceive the burden of regulation as greater than do their male counterparts, and they may be less inclined to want to navigate the time-consuming procedures associated with formalization.

Although the government has made positive progress on licensing reform, the Business Activities Registration Act of 2007 is problematic in some areas, particularly in relation to inspections and penalties and duplicative information provision requirements. There is a need for ongoing review of this act. Under the BEST Program, the government is working on the design of a new draft policy on sector licensing (box 2.2). It is also working on the establishment of a national registry linking business start-up requirements and licensing, to be accessed at a level of government closest to the user, and proposals for improving interagency coordination.

The proposed reform, which embraces international best practice, could substantially contribute to lowering business entry barriers in Tanzania.

Box 2.2

Proposed Draft Policy on Licensing

- Limits regulation strictly to areas where there is a clear necessity to preserve national security, key economic and strategic interests, public health, safety, the environment, and natural resources
- Delinks the revenue and regulatory functions of licensing
- Harmonizes licensing with other aspects of the start-up process
- Repeals the Industrial Licensing Act
- Removes the requirement for firms licensed under sector laws to also have a general business license

Source: DAI Europe (2006).

Closing a Business Is Very Expensive

A well functioning system to deal with companies and individuals that get into financial difficulties is vital to a modern market economy, but Tanzania's current procedures are inefficient and expensive by international standards. Unviable businesses can linger for years, preventing assets and human capital from being reallocated to more productive uses and viable companies can be denied an opportunity to reorganize themselves effectively and trade out of debt. Findings of the MKURABITA diagnostic team reveal that to close a company voluntarily costs US$2,750. This is almost four times the average annual wage for an ordinary Tanzanian.

In many developing countries, bankruptcy is so inefficient that creditors hardly ever use it. But a malfunctioning bankruptcy system can help to encourage a nonrepayment culture, commercial immorality, and irresponsible trading. Moreover, an efficient business closure system can promote improved access to credit. This is because lenders have greater certainty they will recover a high proportion of their funds within a reasonable time and at a reasonable cost in the event of a business failure, and therefore have a greater incentive to lend. Such a system can also help an entrepreneur who has got himself or herself into financial difficulty to make a fresh start. Unfortunately, Tanzania's insolvency procedures rank poorly in comparison with those of competitor countries.[4]

Insolvency procedures are still used very sparingly in mainland Tanzania. In Zanzibar, no insolvency cases have been reported since Zanzibar achieved independence in 1964. The reasons for this are unclear: it may be due to limited access to justice, inefficiencies or lack of confidence in the court system, cultural factors, or the fact that by international standards, the procedures are complex, technical and therefore costly. MKURABITA reports that the winding up procedure in Zanzibar takes an average of 571 days and costs on average US$3,891 (Institute for Liberty and Democracy 2005).

Key Recommendations

- Consider the introduction of best practice models for company formation and operation that provide simplified, low-cost procedures and reporting requirements applicable to small companies;
- Conduct targeted information campaigns for women that focus on the benefits of, and processes associated with, company incorporation.
- Design and implement a policy on sector licensing that (i) limits regulation strictly to areas where there is a clear necessity to preserve

national security, key economic and strategic interests, public health, safety, the environment, and natural resources; (ii) delinks the revenue and regulatory functions of licensing (iii) harmonizes licensing with other aspects of the start-up process; (iv) repeals the Industrial Licensing Act; (v) removes the requirement for firms licensed under sector laws to also hold a general business license; and (vi) establishes a code of conduct on best practices to eliminate licensing bureaucracy.

- Establish a business registry system that is accessible at the local level, and which features (i) links to other registries involved in business start-up; (ii) provision of information to businesses on relevant fees, levies, regulations, compliance standards, and contact points in sectoral ministries; (iii) provision of relevant application forms; and (iv) provision of notice to the relevant district administration and sectoral agencies on the business.
- Establish time limits for the granting of administrative approvals, standardize and simplify forms, provide widespread information in Kiswahili on business entry procedures and any changes.
- Ensure all baseline and M&E data are sex disaggregated to better measure gender impacts.

Notes

1. Interview by GEM team, January 2007.
2. Tanzania's new Companies Act replaced the Companies Act Cap 212 of 1929, which was based on English company law of the time.
3. "Studies have concluded that the regulatory implications of the existing business licensing system contributed largely to the persistence of a large informal sector accounting for 70 percent of all employment and the continued failure of initiatives to stimulate the development and growth of the formal sector" (Maajar, Rwechungura, Nguluma & Makami 2003, p10).
4. World Bank (2006a): (i) it takes on average 3 years to complete insolvency proceedings in Tanzania, in contrast to Uganda's 2 years and Ireland's 4 months; and (ii) creditors can expect on average to recover only around 22 percent of the money they are owed, in contrast to nearly 93 percent in Japan.

CHAPTER 3

Access to Land and Site Development

"When I needed land my brothers refused to give it to me because I was married. In my culture a woman has to be a vessel, and respect her wifely, motherly, and grandmotherly duties. Women are not expected to own property."

—Khadija Simba (Kay), Kay's Hygiene Products
Voices of Women Entrepreneurs in Tanzania

Property Rights

What Is It About Property Rights That Makes Them So Important?

Land in Tanzania is vital because of the predominance of agriculture within the economy, the centrality of agriculture to poverty reduction,[1] and its importance in providing collateral for business finance. As noted in chapter 1, agriculture is an important source of employment for 84 percent of economically active women and 80 percent of economically active men (Blackden and Rwebangira 2004). More than 46 percent of GDP and 54.2 percent of export earnings are generated by the agricultural sector, made up mainly of smallholder farms[2] that depend on family labor, and particularly on women in the areas of food crop production, marketing, and processing of agricultural products (90 percent).[3]

Approximately 98 percent of economically active rural women are engaged in agriculture. Traditionally women are responsible for almost all livestock activities of dairy husbandry. In Zanzibar they constitute 74 percent of the labor force in agroenterprises and predominate in onshore fisheries. Women carry out most of the weeding, harvesting, transportation, threshing, processing, and storage activities, and they are also responsible for preparing food, fetching water, and gathering firewood.[4]

Despite this contribution, women are estimated to own only one-fifth, or about 19 percent of titled land in Tanzania, with an average land holding size of 0.21–0.30 ha, compared to 0.61–0.70 ha for men (Bureau of Statistics 1994). Women also have very limited access to production resources. Ninety-one percent of women farmers in Zanzibar North, for example, do not use agricultural inputs at all, 86 percent do not have access to formal means of credit, and 80 percent have no access to extension services (figure 3.1). Since men tend to carry out most of the marketing activities, women do not have control over the proceeds of their labor.

Insecure land rights discourage women from making the necessary investments in their land that would increase its productivity and economic value. If claims to land are uncertain, households living at the margin are unlikely to see the value of—or feel they can afford—investing scarce resources in soil quality, irrigation systems, or higher value crops that require expensive inputs or offer delayed economic returns.[5] Likewise, if claims to land are uncertain, the vulnerability of households to shocks or economic distress can be much greater than for those households with secure land rights.

Why Do So Few Women Have Control over Land?
Cultural and Customary Norms Relating to Use and Inheritance of Land—In contrast to neighboring Kenya and Uganda, formal legal rights

Figure 3.1. Female Farmers in Zanzibar North—Access to Productive Resources

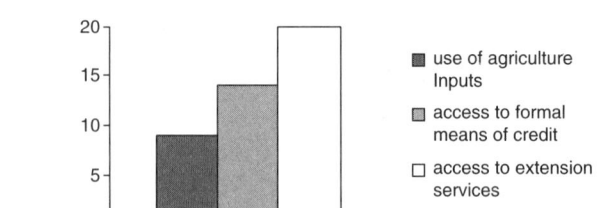

Source: FAO (1997).

protecting women's ownership of and access to land in Tanzania are strong. The right for both women and men to own land and property is embodied in Article 23 of the Tanzanian constitution—women, like men, may hold, own, and dispose of property lawfully obtained. Other legislation also provides relatively strong legal protection for women landowners (box 3.1).

Box 3.1

Land: Formal Legal Rights for Women

- The **National Land Policy** states: *"In order to enhance and guarantee women's access to land and security of tenure, women will be entitled to acquire land in their own right not only through purchase but also through allocation. However, inheritance of clan or family land will continue to be governed by custom and tradition, provided they are not contrary to the constitution and the principles of natural justice."*

- The constitutional right for women to own land is embodied in the **Law of Marriage Act** and the **Land Acts**. Part II Section 3(2) of the Land Act states "the right of every woman to acquire, hold, use and deal with land shall, to the same extent and subject to the same restrictions, be treated as the right of any man."[6] The act states that occupancy cannot be surrendered in order to defeat the rights of a spouse.

- The **Village Land Act** invalidates customary laws that discriminate against women, and recognizes a wife's rights to land on the death of a spouse or on divorce. It provides that "any rule of customary law or any such decision in respect of land held under customary tenure shall be void and inoperative and shall not be given effect to by any authority, to the extent to which it denies women, children or persons with a disability lawful access to ownership, occupation or use of any such land." The act also provides for allocation to women of a certain number of places on the Village Adjudication Committees and **Village Land Councils,** which have decision-making responsibilities concerning occupancy rights and land disputes. By law, both spouses must be registered[a] and mortgages can only be issued with the consent of the spouse or spouses, who are entitled to a copy of the mortgage agreement.

Source: Authors.
a. Section 161(1) of the Land Act states that where one spouse obtains land under a right of occupancy for co-occupation and use by both spouses, there is a presumption that spouses are occupiers in common, and the Registrar must register this accordingly.

Despite the protection given to women under the formal legal system, in practice customary norms that protect clan land from alienation outside the clan[7] and traditionally vest control of property in men, continue to influence decisions and practices concerning ownership and control of, and access to, land, particularly in rural areas. Since women traditionally lack control over property during their marriage, if their husband dies it is not uncommon, particularly in rural areas, for the husband's relatives to take the family property, including land, homes, livestock, furniture, and household items, and leave the widow and her children without support.[8] According to the MKURABITA Diagnostic (Institute for Liberty and Democracy 2005), the practice of assigning rights of occupancy and decisions on customary inheritance "are taken as part of the collective memory of the community and often reflect the application of customs that discriminate against women despite the existence of laws that prohibit this type of practice."

Property Rights on The Death of a Spouse Can Deprive Women and Their Children of Household and Family Resources—Inheritance in Tanzania is governed by various legal regimes, including customary, Islamic, and statutory laws, which for the most part[9] tend to disproportionately favor male heirs.[10] Customary laws of inheritance are applicable to indigenous patrilineal societies that make up 80 percent of Tanzania's communities.

> The law of inheritance is a contradiction in terms. A widow has a choice between three evils, to be inherited as a wife, to go back to 'her people' or to live where her children have decided, all of which require her to be a dependent irrespective of the number of years she has lived with her now deceased husband, and contributed to the family wealth. This kind of law does not only condemn women to greater poverty in old age, it is counter-productive as it robs them of the moral strength to think beyond subsistence. What a wasted resource! (Rwebangira 1996)

In rural areas, inheritance accounts for the vast majority of land acquisition, but customary law[11] prevents women from inheriting land if there are male heirs, for fear that they may transfer land outside the clan through marriage, and ensures that they do not have the right of residence on family land if they are widowed. Widows are allowed to choose to be inherited by and marry their deceased husband's kin, or to return to their own people, or to live where their children have been allocated a right of residence. Wife inheritance, originally designed as a form of social protection, and to secure a woman's access to land through her husband's brother, is giving rise to serious vulnerability and health issues associated with HIV/AIDS.

Customary laws of inheritance, originally designed to protect wives and children on the death of a husband and father, are now leading to widespread deprivation and poverty. Tying a widow's rights to those of her children brings conflicts in real life, as in the case of polygamous marriages, childlessness, or when the children are daughters, as both the children and the women as mothers are affected. Invariably such practices deprive women and their children of household and family resources and exacerbate poverty among widows. From an economic standpoint, these practices may discourage women from long-term economic investments in the marriage.

Efforts to reform the customary law of inheritance have been underway since 1983 but have been stalled in the process of consensus-building among stakeholders. Government is understandably reluctant to force through reforms to laws and practices that have their roots in strongly held traditional, cultural, and religious values. That said, the landmark High Court decision in *Bernado Ephrahim v. Holaria Pastory*[12] which confirmed as discriminatory and unconstitutional the customary law[13] barring women heirs from disposing of clan land by sale while men could, serves as a reminder that attitudes are changing.

Property Rights During Marriage—Uncertainty with Regard to Indirect Financial Contributions—The Law of Marriage Act 1971, which in theory supersedes customary and Islamic laws,[14] gives women the right to retain and control their own property whether they acquired it before or during their marriage. The act (s.60) also provides that where any property is acquired during the marriage in the name of either the husband or the wife, the presumption is that that property belongs absolutely to that person to the exclusion of the other spouse. This means that if the house is in the name of the husband, which it is in the vast majority of cases, the presumption is that the property is owned by the husband, unless the wife is able to prove she has contributed to its acquisition. This can be problematic, especially where the woman's contribution has been nonfinancial.[15] Moreover, given the strong cultural inhibition against women holding property in their own name or even jointly with the husband, and the fact that properties are invariably registered in the name of the husband, this provision can operate to dispossess women of their property rights.

Ability to Dispose of Family Home without Knowledge of Spouse—In theory, during the marriage, the law protects the rights of a spouse living in a matrimonial home that is owned by the other spouse by preventing the sale or disposal of the home in the absence of consent from the nonowning spouse (box 3.2). But in reality these provisions operate only to the extent that a wife knows about them and is prepared to enforce them. Spousal, family, or community coercion; a fear of alienation; low education levels; poverty; a perception that discriminatory practices may prevail in the justice machinery; and a culture of nonassertiveness can often combine to defeat the protections offered by the act.

Property Rights on Divorce—Uncertainties with Regard to the Influence of Custom and In Estimating the Extent of Contributions In Kind—The Law of Marriage Act sets out the rules that apply upon the grant of a separation or divorce, to the division of property acquired by a couple during the marriage by their joint efforts (box 3.3). The court is required to have regard "to the extent of the contributions made by each party in money, property or work towards the acquiring of the assets but discriminatory attitudes tend to undervalue domestic services performed by a wife, and sometimes perpetuate a need for 'concrete evidence' in the form of receipts to prove a wife's entitlement." Moreover, the court is

---

Box 3.2

Formal Rights of a Nonowning Spouse over the Matrimonial Home

Section 59 of the Law of Marriage Act prevents an owning spouse from disposing or in some other way alienating the home without the consent of the other partner while the marriage subsists. The nonowner spouse is said to have an interest in the home capable of being protected by "caveat," and any sale or disposition will be deemed to be subject to the right of the other spouse to continue to reside in the matrimonial home until (i) the marriage is dissolved; or (ii) the court orders otherwise.[a] This provision also applies to desertion and provides that the deserting spouse cannot evict the other spouse from the home without a court order.

Source: Authors.
a. Unless the person acquiring the estate or interest can satisfy the court that he had no notice of the interest of the other spouse, and could not by the exercise of reasonable diligence have become aware of it.

Box 3.3

Rights on Divorce under the Law of Marriage Act

Under the Law of Marriage Act, the court has the power, when granting or after granting a separation or divorce, to order the division of any assets acquired by the couple during the marriage by their joint efforts, or to order the sale of any such asset and division of the proceeds between the couple. In arriving at its determination, the court is required to, among other things, have regard "to the customs of the community to which the parties belong." It must also have regard to "the extent of the contributions made by each party in money, property, or work towards the acquiring of the assets," "the needs of the children, and subject to those considerations, shall incline towards equality of division."[a] Four issues are presented by this section:

- The fact that the court is required to take into account the customs of the community to which the parties belong
- The interpretation of the word "work" in determining the extent of the contributions made by each party toward acquisition of matrimonial assets— whether, for example, tilling the plot in the village would be considered "work" toward acquiring a residence in an urban center
- The status of indirect financial contributions
- Accurately estimating the extent of the parties' contributions, especially where contributions "in kind" are measured against easily quantified financial contributions. There is a possibility that, where such contribution by the wife is in-kind (staying at home and taking care of the family while the husband goes to work), this might not be considered to be an equal contribution "towards acquiring the assets."

a. For the purposes of this section, references to assets acquired during the marriage include assets owned before the marriage by one party that have been substantially improved during the marriage by the other party or by their joint efforts.

required[16] to take into account the customs of the community to which the parties belong. In addition, because of lack of awareness and traditional nonassertiveness on the part of women, customary norms often prevail at the end of the day.[17] Although women in most urban areas have won court orders for division of matrimonial assets, such orders are rare in rural areas where customary law dictates remain strong, despite not having legal force. Unfortunately discriminatory rules under the Customary Law (Declaration) Order of 1963,[18] although overridden by the Law of

Marriage Act, continue to influence people's understanding about women's entitlement to property and support upon divorce. In some cases, women who have been awarded a division of land in rural areas have been prevented from implementing such orders.[19] Case law appears increasingly to support women in these circumstances, but the situation remains unclear (box 3.3).

For nonmarried cohabiting couples, the situation is also uncertain. Section 160 of the Law of Marriage Act states that "where it is proved that a man and woman have lived together for two years or more, in such circumstances as to have acquired the reputation of being husband and wife, there shall be a rebuttable presumption that they were duly married." However, whereas s.160(2) talks of rights to maintenance, custody, and other relief upon a separation, rights to property are not specifically mentioned, which leaves the position uncertain.

Problems with Formalization of Occupation Rights—For a property rights system to function efficiently, rights must be able to be fixed by registration in a modern and reliable system that can be accessed by any

---

Box 3.4

Case Laws Upholding Women's Property Rights

The court has held in the case of *Bi Hawa Mohamed v. Ally Seifu* that domestic duties and care amount to a "contribution" within the provisions of the LMA.[a] But the position continues to remain uncertain with regard to indirect financial contributions, that is, where the spouse uses her money to take care of other aspects of the family needs, such as food and clothing. Further, it is not universally accepted that the performance of domestic duties entitles a wife to an equal division. In the case of *Hamida Abdul v. Ramadhani Mwakaje*,[b] Bahati J. held that while he accepted that *Bi Hawa's* case is authority for the proposition that domestic services amount to a contribution under the act, this does not necessarily mean they amount to an *equal* contribution. In that case, the judge upheld an award to the wife of T Sh 50,000 as "a fair and reasonable amount. Apart from these domestic services, there is no evidence to show the contribution by the wife towards the acquisition of the house."

Source: Authors.
a. *Bi Hawa Mohamed v. Ally Seifu* [1983] TLR.
b. Civil Appeal No. 12 of 1998.

individual or economic agent. In Tanzania, there are two legal systems for formalizing real estate property: (1) statutory law (regulated by the Land Act of 1999, which applies to urban areas), and (2) customary law (regulated by the Village Land Act of 1999, which applies to rural areas and village lands). In both cases, the rights granted are rights of occupancy. Two registration systems coexist, one for general lands under the Office of the Registrar of Titles and one for village lands, which is administered by the village councils and supervised by the Office of the Registrar of Titles. Securing formal title under either is difficult. Although the process of registration is an opportunity for women to assert their interest in land, only a very small percentage of land is registered and the system is both costly and inaccessible.

Formal access to urban property is conditional on the fulfillment of development and planning schemes that are difficult to establish. This means that most urban dwellers live in "unplanned areas" where there are no clear rules regulating land use, where property rights are insecure, and where transference of title in practice requires the approval of the Commissioner for Lands. For businesses to purchase land and a building in the periurban area of Dar es Salaam, the law requires 12 procedures costing 61 days in processing time and 12.6 percent of the property's value. In all, six different Tanzanian government officials are involved in the property transfer (World Bank 2005a).

With regard to customary rights of occupancy, the key issue for women is that they are not afforded the same customary rights of occupancy as men because of the strong cultural inhibition against women holding property in their own name or even jointly with their husbands. This fact, together with traditional attitudes that still strongly influence village decision making bodies and other authorities with regard to land, discourages women from applying for the grant of right of occupancy in their own names in the first place. The documentation and registration process for customary rights of occupancy is very recent—only 12 or so villages have initiated one, and only around 4 percent of owners in these villages have obtained a Certificate of Customary Right of Occupancy (Institute for Liberty and Democracy 2005).

Where land registration has taken place, women are not commonly registered as owners and their rights are not noted on the title. The s.161 Land Act protection requiring that both spouses be registered as co-owners does not apply to village land, and the law does not require certificates of customary rights to carry the names of both spouses (a recommendation of the Land Commission that was not carried forward into the acts). Although the Village Land Act s.30 prevents the village council from consenting to an assignment of a customary right of occupancy if it would be likely to operate "to defeat the right of any woman to occupy land under the customary right of occupancy, a derivative right or as a successor in title to the assignor," this provision is not completely fool-proof. Women need to be strongly encouraged to ensure their customary occupation rights are protected by way of a registerable instrument such as a caveat.

There is evidence that establishing women's rights to land under the land acts at the village level has been problematic, with reluctance being shown in some districts. Where village land councils have been established, women's representation is not always as stipulated in the. law, and there have been cases of women sitting on adjudication organizations alongside their husbands and relatives, choosing to remain silent for fear of contradicting male relatives (Oxfam, Trocaire, and Concern 2005).

Dispute settlement is also problematic, mainly because of resource, technical, and capacity constraints. Although many issues hindering formalization of property rights will be addressed under various components of the World Bank Competitiveness Project, which will provide technical assistance and capacity building to develop efficient land registration and administration services,[20] critical issues for women, as discussed above, remain.

Site Development Constraints—The current city plan for Dar es Salaam is unduly restrictive, particularly in relation to the location of small businesses. Because no provision is made for informal sector activities in city and municipal plans, women entrepreneurs are constantly harassed by police and military officers, even though they may be performing a service highly valued by the community, such as food vending (Mama Lishe). Whereas the Land Act provides for right of occupancy of an industrial plot, there are no specific areas marked in development plans for small operators, and no provisions in town planning law requiring the compulsory designation in district plans for informal operators. In addition, site development approvals can take a long time to finalize (Coopers and Lybrand 1997).

Prioritized actions under the BEST Program seek to address lack of transparency in the site development process by detailing procedures and timings for inspections, permits, and site approvals, and methods of redress for failure to comply with specified customer service targets. Likewise, the SME policy commits to putting the following strategies in place: (i) allocation and development of land for SMEs by local authorities, (ii) development of industrial clusters and trading centers, and (iii) identification and allocation of underutilized public buildings to SMEs.

Key Recommendations

- *Strengthening of enforcement.* Strengthen enforcement of land laws and the dissemination of knowledge about women's property rights, on why land is a valuable resource, and on other resources available to mortgage loans. Disseminate training manuals aimed at magistrates and customary leaders and information leaflets aimed at the community that records statute and case law establishing women's entitlement to property and support upon the death of, or divorce from, a spouse—to reduce cultural inhibitions and traditional attitudes preventing women from accessing justice. Centers should be established in rural areas where women entrepreneurs could access relevant information for their businesses.

- *Simplification of land laws.* Support widespread dissemination of simplified versions of the land laws.

- *Property rights during marriage.* Consideration could be given to amending s.60 Law of Marriage Act (Mainland) to provide that property acquired during the marriage in the name of either the husband or the wife belongs to both spouses unless the contrary is established. This would be in conformity with s.161 of the Land Act of 1999 and would prevent husbands from dealing separately with matrimonial property, but might also discourage women from acquiring separate property during the marriage. Views could be canvassed regarding this issue.

- *Property laws on the death of a spouse.* Tanzania's (Mainland) laws on inheritance should be reviewed and repealed as appropriate, to create a uniform law of inheritance, and bring the law into line with the constitution, CEDAW, and CRC. Consideration could be given to the concept of giving a widow a life interest in the matrimonial home, protecting the ability of a widow to stay in the matrimonial home during her lifetime while allowing the land to revert to the husband's clan on her death.

- *Property rights on divorce.* Review the requirement in Section 114 (2) Law of Marriage Act (Mainland) which obliges a court to have regard to the customs of the community to which the parties belong. The law could provide that a court should have regard to the customs of the community to which the parties belong, so long as they are not inconsistent with the constitution. In addition, instead of having regard to the extent of the contributions made by each party in money, property, or work toward acquiring matrimonial assets, the court could be required to have regard to extent of the contributions made by each party to the marriage (including acquisition of matrimonial assets), and to the care of the family.

- *Site development.* Review town planning legislation to ensure provision of a compulsory requirement that serviced workspace for micro- and small-scale enterprises be earmarked and set aside in urban areas.

Notes

1. The *Participatory Poverty Assessment* highlights the importance of agriculture for poverty reduction: "a remarkable 47 percent of all responses about the causes of poverty were related to being able to farm productively."

2. Approximately 85 percent of Tanzania's arable land is used by smallholders who operate between 0.2 and 2 hectares and traditional agropastoralists who keep an average of 50 head of cattle. It is estimated that the average per capita land holding is only 0.12 ha.

3. Blackden and Rwebangira (2004), and ILO (2001), which notes that women are said to produce 60–80 percent of the country's cash and food crops.

4. Sustainable Development Department, FAO, United Nations: http://www.fao.org/waicent/faoinfo/sustdev/WP/direct/WPre0010.htm.

5. In different parts of the developing world secure title to land has been positively correlated with agricultural investments and outputs. In Thailand, for example, a study found that gaining title to land induced higher investment in farming capital. As a result, output was 14–25 percent higher on titled land than on untitled land of equal quality.

6. Before the enactment of the Land Act (1999)[6] and the Village Land Act (1999) women's rights to dispose of land were not equal to those of men. They were restricted by customary law, which dictated that women could not dispose of clan land, whereas men could. The courts have declared such a rule as inconsistent with the constitution and therefore invalid. See *Bernardo Ephrahim v. Holaira Pastory & Gervas Kaizilege* Civil Appeal Court No. 70 of 1989 as per Mwalusanya J on rule 20 of CLDO, 1963.

7. The Customary Law (Declaration) Order, No. 4 of 1963.

8. TAWLA (undated) notes it is often the case that a deceased person's relatives seek to inherit the deceased's property without accepting the collateral customary law duty and responsibility associated with the deceased's role as husband and father.

9. The Indian Succession Act, which essentially codifies English common law, is an exception in that it does not make a distinction between male and female heirs, but it is rarely used, particularly by Africans.

10. Under Islamic law, for example, which is applicable to Muslims, a son generally inherits double the share of a daughter.

11. G.N. No. 436 of 1963.

12. HC (PC) Civil Appeal No. 10 of 1989 (unreported).

13. Customary Law Rule 20.

14. Judicature & Application of Laws ordinance, 1961, Cap 453 s.9 (3a).

15. For example, where a wife lives upcountry and tills the land while her husband works in an urban center and acquires property, or where the wife stays at home and takes care of the family while the husband goes to work.

16. Despite the provisions of the Judicature and Application of Laws Ordinance Cap 453 that "the rules of customary law and Islamic law shall not apply in regard to any matter provided for the Law of Marriage Act, 1971."

17. The continuing existence of discriminatory rules under the Customary Law (Declaration) Order of 1963, although overridden by the Law of Marriage Act, continue to influence people's understanding about women's entitlement to property and support upon divorce.

18. Such as Rule 71A which provides that on divorce a peasant's wife is only entitled to one-fourth of a share of the agricultural crops in the year of her divorce, and Rule 74, which states that a husband shall pay maintenance to his former wife only if the husband is the guilty party to the marital breakdown.

19. Bukoba RM's Court Matrimonial Cause no. 1/1991 *Hermelinda Mutarubukwa v. Thadeo Mutarubukwa* (unreported).

20. By reengineering the processes supporting updated legislation, improving the infrastructure for surveying, mapping, and registration, and decentralizing land administration services to the district and village levels in about 15 districts.

CHAPTER 4

Access to Finance

To get a bank loan is difficult for women. The banking process does not favor women. Even if you have collateral, the banks can make problem.

—Shamsa Divani
Voices of Women Entrepreneurs in Tanzania

Constraints of Limited Access to Finance

Limited Access to Finance Constrains All Businesses, But Particularly Those Owned by Women

Lack of access to finance has been identified as the second most debilitating constraint to doing business in Tanzania, falling only marginally behind access to infrastructure (World Bank 2004b). Tanzania is currently ranked 117 out of 175 countries in the cost of doing business league tables, in relation to credit access for businesses. Data from the 2006 FinScope survey indicate that 89 percent of Tanzanians have never held a bank account, 3 percent have previously banked, and only 8 percent are currently banked (figure 4.1). The provision of credit to the private sector, although it has doubled since the late 1990s, is still low, at about 8 percent of GDP, compared with 23 percent in Kenya. According to the 2004 ICS, only 20 percent of enterprises reported having loans from any financial

63

Figure 4.1. Banking Profile in Tanzania

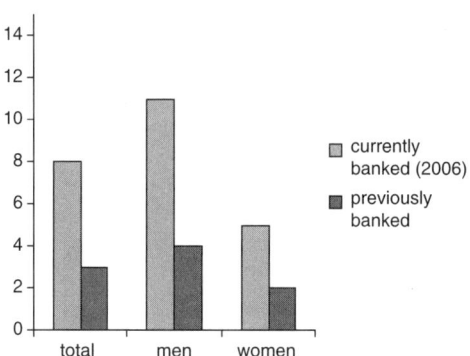

Source: FSDT (2007).

institution, compared with 40 percent in Kenya. In Zanzibar, the situation is worse. Investment Climate Assessment findings show that Zanzibar businesses were far less likely to have loans or overdraft facilities than those on the mainland (World Bank 2004b, 2004c).

The problems are even more significant for MSMEs. A 2003 study estimated that 85 percent of MSMEs do not access any formal sources of credit. A 2004 survey showed that only 6 percent of microenterprises have loans from either microfinance institutions or banks; a 1997 survey showed that only 9 percent of microenterprise requests to banks were granted. These figures suggest that there is probably a large unmet demand for financial services for households and microentrepreneurs in Tanzania. The majority of the economy is working with little formal credit, especially in agriculture and the rural economy, where women predominate.[1] Very limited bank credit is given for agricultural inputs.[2]

Interviews and discussions with women entrepreneurs reveal that access to finance may be an even more serious constraint for them. Their limited control over land affects their ability to secure finance because they are unable to provide collateral for business loans. It is estimated that despite constituting 43 percent of MSMEs, only 5 percent of Tanzanian women are banked. Only 0.53 percent of female-headed, smallholder households access credit (United Republic of Tanzania 2005c). As indicated in figure 4.2, which focuses on SMEs and large limited liability companies, small firms have a harder time getting finance than large ones, and women business owners have a harder time than men (figure 4.2).

According to the FinScope data, men are twice as likely to be banked as women. Only 6 percent of female business owners have any type of banking relationship, compared to 11 percent of male business owners, and the most common type of banking service used by males and females is a savings account (table 4.1).[3] The FinScope data indicate that just one in 10 business owners, male or female, has ever applied for a loan.

Why don't more Tanzanians use loan products? The most commonly cited reasons in the FinScope survey included lack of regular income (63 percent of respondents), lack of money to save (33 percent), and lack of a job (28 percent). Other reasons included lack of knowledge in how to open a bank account, and high bank charges. There appear to be no significant differences between men and women.

Figure 4.2. Difficulty of Getting Credit

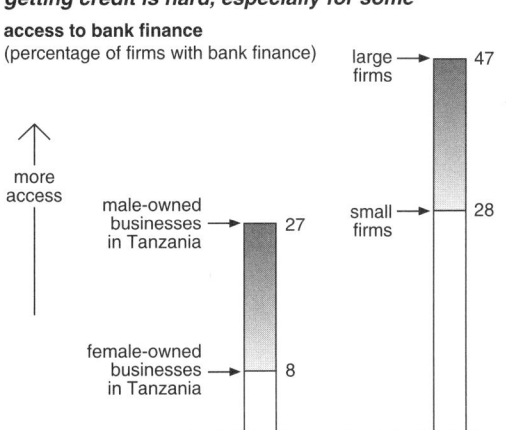

Source: World Bank 2005a.

Table 4.1. Few Women and Men in Tanzania Access Banking Services

Type of banking service	Total	All persons 16–65 (%)		Business owners (%)	
		Men	Women	Men	Women
Savings account	7	9	4	10	5
ATM card	2	3	1	3	1
Postbank account	2	3	1	2	1
Debit card	1	2	1	1	–
Current account	1	1	–	1	1
Fixed deposit	1	1	–	1	–
Total percent banked	8	11	5	11	6

Source: FSDT (2007).
– = not available

The Tanzanian financial system is diverse, but very small in relation to the economy and many of its components are relatively underdeveloped (box 4.1).

MicroCredit Provision Is Still Limited and Not a Complete Solution For Women

According to the FinScope data, about 6 percent of Tanzanians borrow from microfinance institutions. Although solidarity-group lending is a well-established practice, effective individual lending methods, enabling the expansion of microfinance services to established small-scale enterprises, are still underdeveloped.

Microfinance helps the poor, the majority of whom are women, to borrow for business expansion, and to save and buy other relevant products like microinsurance. Research on microcredit initiatives targeted at women shows that improving access to credit for women in developing countries enables them to improve their standard of living. They also have superior credit repayment records compared to men, and lending to women has a greater effect on household welfare than credit directed toward male borrowers (Stotsky 2006).

Additional research broadens the social implications. Anecdotal evidence that the benefits of microfinance can extend beyond the purely economic is beginning to show in formal studies (box 4.2). For example, a recent HIV/AIDS trial in South Africa found definite links between poverty, violence, and HIV/AIDS—incidences of intimate partner violence were

---

Box 4.1

Tanzania's Financial System

Tanzania has 20 licensed banks, 11 nonbank financial institutions, around 650 functioning savings and credit cooperatives (SACCOs), and about 60 NGOs involved in microfinance. Licensed banks dominate the system, but bank deposits amount to only 14 percent of GDP—among the lowest in Sub-Saharan Africa. The Tanzania Postal Savings Bank and several commercial banks (National Microfinance Bank, CRDB, and Akiba Commercial Bank) are the leading providers of microfinance services, with outreach that exceeds the combined outreach of SACCOs and MFIs.

Source: Authors.

Box 4.2

Microfinance Transforming Lives—The Example of the Faraja Trust

The Faraja Microfinance Project was created in the 1990s, when the Faraja Trust ("to comfort" in Swahili) started to rehabilitate sex workers in Morogoro with a high incidence of HIV/AIDS. Dr. Lucy Nkya began to help 450 women in a local brothel, who were mostly widows, abandoned wives, or girls rejected by their families due to early pregnancy. Dr Nkya soon realized that the main problem the women faced in trying to escape prostitution was having no other means to earn a living. "Culturally, here, women are not welcome at home once their husbands have died or abandoned them, so many turn to prostitution as the only option to escape poverty."

Dr. Nkya established the microfinance project to help support the women in starting small-scale income generating activities, such as food and charcoal selling, chicken breeding, and tailoring. Initially, the loans were interest-free, drawing on a fund provided by the Danish aid agency, DANIDA, but today a small interest fee is charged. The project now has more than 3,000 beneficiaries and has created 16 SACCOs in all six districts of the Morogoro region. Some of the women have even managed to purchase land with their profits. "We have found Faraja's loans have not only helped to rehabilitate women who previously had no economic choice other than prostitution, but the chance of HIV/AIDS infection is lowered and children are now more likely to go to school," Dr. Nkya says.

reduced by 55 percent for women given microloans and associated empowerment training, compared to a control group (Pronyk et al. 2006).

Although in 2005 Tanzania amended financial sector laws to recognize a new type of voluntary deposit-taking (and therefore licensed) microfinance institution, called a microfinance company (MFC),[4] the minimum capital requirement of T Sh 800 million for the formation of an MFC is a limiting factor. With the notable exception of PRIDE Tanzania,[5] no other MFIs have found themselves in a position to meet that minimum investment—or indeed many other requirements—which would enable them to apply to the Bank of Tanzania for a license. Knowledgeable in-country sources note that it may take another 2 years before even three MFCs are up and running.[6]

In addition, banking laws constrain the provision of microfinance services in Tanzania. Unsecured loans to a single borrower may not exceed 5 percent of a licensed bank's capital (Radhawa and Gallardo 2003). This limit constrains downscaling by commercial banks into microfinance, and inhibits MFIs from seeking licensing or prudentially supervised status because virtually all microfinance loans are unsecured. It also has an adverse impact on wholesale lending by licensed banks to microfinance NGOs or SACCOs, whose major clients are female microentrepreneurs.

There is concern, too, that the new MFC law requires complex and stringent financial accounting and reporting. This may go beyond the technical capacity and resources of Tanzanian microfinance providers, and therefore restrict entry into the sector.

However, BRAC, the world's largest NGO with some 6 million women clients in Bangladesh, in 2006 opened five branches in Dar es Salaam and Arusha, respectively. Reportedly, these 10 outlets have built up more than 6,000 borrowers and disbursed the equivalent of more than US$600,000 in loans. BRAC started with its tried and tested microcredit product, which involves group-lending to women, and all BRAC branch managers and loan officers are women. Once it has established this product, BRAC intends to roll out an individual microenterprise loan product for both sexes. By the end of the first quarter of 2007 it expects to start operations in Zanzibar, followed by more rural areas beyond the two urban centers.

Savings and Credit Cooperative Organizations (SACCOs)

Barriers such as low population density, infrastructure challenges that deter people from physically accessing financial institutions, a widespread suspicion of formal financial institutions, and poorly trained bank staff contribute to low levels of access to finance in rural areas. Data from the 2006 FinScope survey show that more than one-third of Tanzanians are more than 2 hours away from financial services.

SACCOs,[7] which are the only potential source of credit for many, if not most, rurally based Tanzanians, provide limited credit products, and tend to be small, weak, and a high-risk option. With the exception of CRDB's 220-member SACCO network, they are not linked to the formal financial system. However, the 2006 FinScope survey found that 9 percent of respondents have had a loan from a SACCO, and that women constitute 41 percent of SACCO users.

Although the government has an overseer responsibility for SACCOs, this tends to be more focused on registration and cooperative principles, rather than on financial performance. As a result, SACCOs do not always use standard accounting procedures, regularly maintain their records, or comply fully with audit requirements. They face other problems, too, including lack of capacity and professional management, viability and outreach, and common standards.

Formal Financing

Access to credit from formal institutions depends on the amount of confidence or incentives lenders have to make credit available. Three factors help to build this confidence: (i) use of collateral to secure a loan (this is commonly known as the security interest); (ii) legal protections that safeguard a lender's security interest; and (iii) the amount of credit information available to the lender (this enables them to assess the risk involved in providing credit to a business). Incentives to lend to government rather than the private sector can have a debilitating effect on the supply of credit to businesses. In Tanzania, banks have strong reason to invest in treasury bills, as opposed to loaning to the private sector, because bond interest is tax-free for maturities over 3 years.

Women, in particular, face obstacles in accessing formal sources of credit, as highlighted in the focus group discussions summarized in box 4.3. (See also chapter 3 for a discussion on related legal and cultural barriers that restrict women's land ownership.)

In response to these kinds of problems, the Government of Tanzania has been considering establishing a women's bank. Given the costly nature of such an initiative, it may be more cost- effective to consider working closely with existing commercial banks to ensure they improve their outreach and nondiscriminatory customer service delivery to women. In addition, there are legislative reforms that could disproportionately benefit women's access to finance, including development of efficient, nonmovable securities legislation, asset leasing, and credit information.

Reform of the System for Registration of Securities over Movable Assets

Banks in Tanzania tend to demand title to land as security for loans. This is a practice that effectively denies access to credit not only to nonland-owners, but also to those landowners who do not have formal certificates of title. The majority of Tanzanians fall into this category, including most small business people and most women. De Soto estimates that

Box 4.3

Tanzanian Women's Constraints to Accessing Finance

Recent discussions with women entrepreneurs confirm that access to finance for women is hindered mainly by supply-side constraints:

- The demand for collateral is a major barrier for women, few of whom own land.
- Many small business owners (women, in particular) fear banking conditions and are reluctant even to approach a bank to inquire or solicit loans.
- Loan approval for any business is linked to obtaining a tax identification number (TIN). Obtaining a TIN is considered to be a lengthy, cumbersome, and often corrupt process.
- Banks require access to business records, including annual turnover figures, before a loan application is considered. Most SMEs do not keep such records or do not have bank accounts.
- Costly loan application and approval processes discourage clients from soliciting loans from formal banks.
- Lack of follow-up from banks once the loan is issued was cited as a problem. "Banks care only about repayment of their loans and not the client's needs and business problems."
- Lack of familiarity with techniques to circumvent Islamic prohibitions on borrowing and paying interest. Some women mentioned that their husbands prohibit them from borrowing so that they remain faithful to their Islamic beliefs. However, there are legitimate ways of borrowing through male relatives—techniques with which Tanzanian men tend not to be familiar. "These are some of the techniques we need training in here for us and for our men," one woman participant noted.
- Lack of suitable women-friendly products, such as leasing.
- Lack of tailored or structured business development services to enable SMEs, particularly women with start-up businesses, to break through the red tape of the commercial banking sector.
- Discriminatory attitudes by bank officials may discourage women from approaching a bank.
- Some corrupt practices such as bank staff requiring additional fees or other payments before approving or disbursing loans within an acceptable amount of time for the borrower.

Source: Based on focus group discussions with women entrepreneurs, Dar es Salaam, October 2006.

86 percent of all urban property and 97 percent of all businesses in urban areas, valued at US$11.6 billion, is held outside the legal system and therefore cannot be used to create more wealth (Institute for Liberty and Democracy 2005).

The problem is compounded for women who are not generally named or do not have their interests in land registered on land titles for the following reasons:[8]

- Land that is not surveyed is not accepted as collateral by banks, even if it is formalized under the new system of MKURABITA
- While the Village Land Registry is being implemented, the only alternative for the majority of rural property owners is to convert a customary right of occupancy into a statutory right of occupancy. This means surveying the area at a cost of more than US$900, so that they may apply for granted rights of occupancy in rural areas;[9]
- Even when applicants have surveyed land, it cannot be used as collateral until it is formalized—an extremely lengthy and costly process. The applicant is responsible for all costs and time involved in the verification and valuation process between the bank and the Ministry of Land.
- Matrimonial property, surveyed or not, cannot be used as collateral by women without the consent of their husbands, which is almost never given for a woman-solicited loan.

In developed economies, assets other than land are commonly used as collateral for loans. These come in many different forms, ranging from stock or machinery to less tangible property such as patents. By international standards, Tanzania has a complicated, outdated, and nontransparent legal framework relating to the use of nonland assets as collateral for loans (box 4.4). On the mainland, pledging a movable property such as a car takes 297 days, whereas in Zanzibar such pledges are nonexistent (Institute for Liberty and Democracy 2005).

To be fully protected in law, a security interest must be registered with one of two registers. The first is for use by companies and is administered by BRELA; the second is for noncompanies and is administered by the Registrar of Documents in the Ministry of Lands.[10] Sometimes chargees find it necessary to register in both places—the charge itself with BRELA and the documents giving effect to the charge at the Registry of Documents. In theory, such a system should foster confidence amongst

Box 4.4

Problems with the Chattels Transfer Act

- A lack of transparent linkages between the two separate registers means inadequate protection for lenders.
- Informal arrangements that create nonland security interests, such as handing over some equipment as a deposit for a loan, cannot be registered in Tanzania and cannot be protected.
- Register search is difficult, because there is no alphabetical indexing by reference to the surname of the grantor.
- Manual registration systems impose delays in registration, which means that the provision of finance is delayed. Manual registration also affords considerable scope for human error.
- Technical legal documents, which are costly and time-consuming to obtain, are required to enable registration (and therefore protection) of security interests.

Source: World Bank (2003).

lenders by providing a mechanism for protecting their security interests and obtaining useful credit information.[11]

Tanzania's old manual and uncoordinated system of registering nonland securities is inappropriate for the 21st century. A single, comprehensive registration system for movable assets would provide protection for secured financiers; information for third parties, particularly financiers who are contemplating the provision of credit to a borrower, and the mechanics for establishing a system of priorities between secured creditors (box 4.5). For women who are denied access to land as a means of collateral, and who are disproportionately affected by time-consuming, costly procedures, the importance of such a reform is particularly profound.

Asset Leasing

Asset leasing helps businesses acquire immediate possession of capital assets with which to generate income. For this they pay by installments (with interest) until the asset is paid off. Asset leasing has been successful internationally in generating significantly increased levels of capital investment by businesses. It can allow new businesses with limited start-up capital and

Box 4.5

Benefits of Secured Transactions Reform

In 1999 Romania undertook best practice secured transactions reform. The number of borrowers increased threefold and the volume of credit by 50 percent. In Slovakia a similar reform resulted in more than 70 percent of new business credit being secured by non-land-secured transactions.

Source: World Bank (2005a).

short-term cash flow potential to start operating immediately.[12] It achieves this by matching repayments with the cash flow patterns of the lessee, and by allowing lessees to conserve the limited capital they might have.[13] For smaller businesses, which cannot access or afford traditional lending as easily as larger companies, and for nonland owners who have no security to offer, the impact of asset leasing has been particularly significant.

For Tanzanian women entrepreneurs who struggle with discriminatory treatment when it comes to accessing credit, and who tend not to have access to land and property to be offered as collateral, the potential offered by leasing could be considerable (box 4.6). The Government of Tanzania recognizes the value of leasing in supporting the growth of the SME sector, and has committed in its SME Development Policy (United Republic of Tanzania 2002b) to enhancing financial reforms by promoting leasing, among other things.[14]

The opportunities for leasing to support increased access to finance for Tanzanians are promising (box 4.7), but again, regulatory obstacles constrain the growth of the industry in Tanzania,[15] particularly with regard to servicing SMEs. The total portfolio of the leasing market in Tanzania is around US$3.2 million, which is less than 2 percent of GDP. There are currently four major banks and three other companies offering leasing or some form of asset financing. With the exception of the banks, leasing practitioners in Tanzania are small operations with limited resources and low net worth (IFC 2005).

Issues standing in the way of leasing growth in Tanzania can be grouped into the following categories: (i) an inadequate legal framework governing leasing, including problems associated with judicial interpretation of rights and obligations under lease contracts, enforcing lease contracts, and repossession of leased assets; (ii) inadequate tax incentives to encourage

Box 4.6

Advantages of Leasing Offers

From the government's perspective:

- Leasing expands productivity by enabling new and small firms to access financing for investment.
- A leasing industry broadens competition in financial services, and produces a livelier and more competitive capital market to help finance firms of all sizes and sectors. It should also produce a more stable business sector in that sources of external finance are diversified and competitive. In addition, by facilitating the financing of imported capital equipment, leasing companies can help transfer technology to domestic industries.

At the firm level:

- Leasing ensures dedicated use of funds, because the lessor purchases the equipment directly from the supplier, leaving no opportunity for the lessee to use the funds for other purposes.
- The firm's broader finances are not put at risk by leasing, in contrast to debt, which involves taking wider security over the firm's assets.
- Cash flow, not credit history or collateral, is the focus in determining whether an applicant for asset leasing will be successful.
- Repayment patterns can be custom designed to match the lessee's cash flow.
- Leasing offers flexibility with regard to the period for which the finance is provided.

Source: Authors.

new entrants (and therefore increased competition) to the leasing sector; (iii) unfavorable VAT treatment of lease finance; and (iv) lack of public awareness of leasing. Given the difficulties that SMEs and women face accessing traditional sources of lending, the importance of such stumbling blocks cannot be understated.

However, positive efforts are underway. For example, the Financial Sector Deepening Trust (FSDT), launched in 2005, is channeling donor resources to support the development of pro-poor financial markets, with the aim of achieving greater access to the financial sector in Tanzania for more people. The trust helps smaller financial firms, especially microfinance institutions and small banks, develop into sustainable,

Box 4.7

Sero Lease and Finance—Demonstrating the Benefits of Leasing

A veterinarian by profession, Dr. Victoria Kisyombe founded Sero Lease and Finance Ltd. in response to the problems facing women microentrepreneurs, mainly widows with limited means to earn a living in rural areas. "We went into this because most women lack collateral. We decided to look at leasing as our main product," Dr. Kisyombe says. Sero Lease offers financial leasing products, lending funds for equipment that becomes the property of the client once all payments are made. Incorporated in 2002 as a limited liability company, Sero Lease has 28 employees and more than 3,000 exclusively female clients, with an average loan amount of T Sh 500,000 (around US$500) and a 99 percent payback rate. "Before we lease out anything, we sit down with the women. We give them the opportunity to make sure they understand what credit is all about," says Dr. Kisyombe. Sero Lease also runs a not-for-profit training center through the Sero Businesswomen Association (SEBA) that provides basic business and bookkeeping skills, as well as sensitization programs on HIV/AIDS and legal issues facing women entrepreneurs. Initially supported by various donors, Sero Lease has received significant loan financing, including from international sources. However, finance still remains a key issue for the organization. "It has not been easy. We had a long road to travel until we were trusted and were able to borrow. Even now, we cannot borrow the full amount we need. In February 2007 Dr. Kisyombe became the first female client of Exim Bank's new WEF program with a US$1 million loan which will be on lent to as many as 30,000 microentrepreneurs." Dr. Kisyombe's current priorities include lobbying for the passage of a new leasing law, opening additional branches in rural areas, and leasing agricultural equipment.

Source: Cutura (2007).

credible, and creditworthy partners for commercial banks and larger financial institutions.

Women Would Gain from Moves to Enhance Access to Credit Information

An important pillar of the formal credit market is availability of information about the credit-worthiness of borrowers. Such data can be collected by the bank through its dealings with a particular borrower or from a public registry. The public registry serves as a repository for borrowers' performance on a wide range of credit obligations over their lifetime, and is considerably cheaper and more informative than private information.

Tanzania does not perform well in terms of easily obtained information on the creditworthiness of borrowers (table 4.2). This means that women are unable to benefit from their excellent repayment rates as they grow their businesses beyond the capacity of microfinance institutions.

On a positive front, the 2003 amendments to the Bank of Tanzania (BoT) Act empower BoT to create a credit reference database and collect information on the payment records of clients of all banks, financial institutions, savings and credit schemes, and other entities engaged in the extension of credit. The BoT is also authorized to license and regulate the operation of private credit reference bureaus, which may access information from its database. The Central Bank is in the process of identifying ways to create unique identification numbers. It has engaged consultants to work out the details of setting up such a bureau and to investigate the feasibility of incorporating microfinance institutions into a proposed new credit reference system. In addition, the BEST Program is working on the implementation of a National Identity Card System, which could greatly facilitate the process of checking a borrower's credentials and credit history.

Sustaining the Provision of Financial Services to Women in Tanzania Is Crucial

Sustainability in the provision of financial services to the poor is crucial to building the discipline and confidence needed by recipients to move them beyond a subsistence venture. However, the notion of financial sustainability has not been well understood by all government-driven

Table 4.2. International Benchmarking: Doing Business in 2007—Ease of Getting Credit Indicators

Economy	Credit information index (0–6)[a]
Hong Kong, China	5
Zambia	0
Kenya	2
Tanzania	0
Uganda	0

Source: World Bank (2006a).
a. This measures rules affecting the scope, accessibility, and quality of credit information available either through public or private registries. Higher scores indicate the availability of more credit information to facilitate lending decisions.

credit programs, with the result that subsidized credit has, in some cases, undermined the essence of sustainable financial service provision to the poor.[16] The case of the Women's Entrepreneurship Development Fund (WEDF) in Zanzibar is an exception. Three years after initiating the program, it has become a stand-alone, self-sustaining microfinance NGO with outreach in all the 16 districts of Zanzibar.

As part of SME Policy implementation, the government initiated an SME Guarantee Scheme (SME–CGS) in 2005, with the specific objective of providing credit guarantees to financial institutions for short- to medium-term financing of SMEs. Sixteen financial institutions[17] are currently participating in the scheme, which targets SMEs with finance requirements ranging from T Sh 5 million to T Sh 200 million, for 1 to 5 years. Participating institutions guarantee loans on a pro rata basis up to 50 percent of the principal amount, irrespective of the loan tenure. Consultations reveal that the scheme is difficult and costly for banks to use, as a result of which few use it. Guarantees worth T Sh 1 billion have been issued so far, but mainly to medium-size enterprises.

Some entrepreneurs propose that the scheme should be transferred to the SME-oriented Small Industries Development Organization (SIDO) to reduce bureaucracy and take advantage of SIDO's countrywide coverage. A major problem mentioned is the BoT's tendency not to deal with SMEs directly (SME Focus Magazine 2006). In the past, SIDO operated a government-funded hire purchase scheme for small entrepreneurs, which eventually failed because of poor loan recovery. It is now responsible for administering the National Entrepreneurship Development Fund, through which women are reported as having received 50 percent of the loans extended (Institute for Liberty and Democracy 2005).

The real key to improved access to finance for women entrepreneurs lies with commercial banks. Recognizing the opportunities offered by the growing number of women entrepreneurs and catering for their needs provides a win-win situation.

Key Recommendations

- *Reforming the Chattels Transfer Act and some parts of the Companies Act:* Consider reforming the law relating to secured transactions, using, for example, the UNCITRAL model and instituting a computer-based system of registration. Widespread information dissemination on the law and procedures relating to secured transactions would need to accompany this reform.

- Given the costly and time-consuming nature of establishing a new institution to lend to women, encourage existing commercial banks to establish gender-sensitive programs or lines of credit for women entrepreneurs. Bankers should be trained to appropriate products and provide gender-sensitive customer care to female entrepreneurs.
- *Access to Lease Finance*
  - Introduce appropriate enabling leasing legislation that clarifies the rights and responsibilities of the parties, and provides simplified mechanisms for enforcing a lease agreement and repossessing leased assets
  - Review the Hire Purchase Act to ensure that domestic consumer protection controls are not imposed on leasing transactions that involve capital equipment, as opposed to personal property
  - Review the tax treatment of leasing to encourage new entrants to the sector
  - Review the VAT treatment of leasing, so that the application of VAT does not provide a disincentive for both the use and provision of this form of financing
  - The production of a model agreement and explanatory handbook would be helpful in assisting lessors and lessees in framing and understanding their rights and obligations

Notes

1. Poor physical infrastructure—roads and telephones—have made payment and deposit systems costly for those who live in rural areas. Neither banks nor microfinance institutions have made any significant headway in finding secure and cost-effective ways of lending to these areas.

2. For instance, the government-backed Agricultural Inputs Trust Fund has loaned T Sh.17 billion cumulatively since 2002. However, relative to credit provision to other economic sectors, this figure (equivalent to some US$1.4 million in today's terms) is very low.

3. A business owner is defined as someone who reported being self-employed in either agriculture or business within the past month. In this survey, the definition yielded an estimated 3,373,962 female business owners and 2,900,656 male business owners—16 percent and 14 percent, respectively, of the adult population.

4. The law states that an MFC can undertake financial intermediation and their mandate will be to furnish secured and unsecured credit facilities to households, smallholder farmers, and small and microenterprises in rural and urban areas.

5. Consultations in Tanzania revealed that, since it was established at national level in 1993, PRIDE Tanzania has opened 28 branches countrywide, registering 71,986 members, 65 percent of whom are women. PRIDE has issued 967,450 loans, amounting to T Sh 153.9 billion in Tanzania. The loan repayment rate is 95 percent.

6. Interview with Ian Robinson, FSDT.

7. To obtain a loan from a cooperative, the applicant must have been a member of the SACCO for at least 3 months and have two or three guarantors, all of whom must also be SACCO members. Membership is conditional on payment of an upfront entry fee and compulsory acquisition of shares. Generally the maximum loan available is two times the amount saved, which means that if a significant sum of money is required, the applicant must have been saving for a long time. According to MKURABITA, the procedure to access credit with SACCOs involves 17 administrative steps before seven administrative officers, which takes an average of 100 days at a cost of US$51.

8. Group Discussion with women entrepreneurs in Tanzania at an IFC GEM-sponsored workshop in Dar es Salaam (October 2006).

9. Very few owners, particularly the poor, can follow this procedure, because the cost of complying with the surveying requirement is prohibitive. Surveys are more difficult to obtain in rural areas because surveyors' offices are mainly located in urban areas.

10. The Chattels Transfer Ordinance of 1942 governs the registration of all movable properties. This registry is located in and administered by the Land Office.

11. In that the lender (or a prospective purchaser of an asset) is able to verify that there is no other competing claim on the asset being used as security.

12. Since cash flow, as numerous studies and surveys of SMEs in various countries testify, is the key financial constraint upon such firms, these features are extremely important as marketing advantages for lease products and as commercial advantages for SMEs that use lease facilities.

13. The U.K. Finance and Leasing Association carried out a survey of a sample of U.K. FTSE 250 (large and middle-sized listed) companies in 1999, on why they used leasing. Sixty-six percent of the respondents said cash flow advantages ranked first. The proportion was the same for finance lessees as for operating lessees. The proportion would be undoubtedly even higher for micro- and small enterprises.

14. Including financial products for SMEs, such as hire purchase schemes, inventory financing, venture capital SMEs, and saving and credit schemes.

15. IFC (2005)—"The legal framework for leasing in Tanzania is not conducive to the development of the industry, and has been identified by stakeholders as a disincentive to entry into the leasing market."

16. The Women's Development Fund, initiated by the Ministry of Community Development, Gender and Children in 1995 to increase access to finance to poor women, particularly in rural areas, was an unfortunate example.

17. Twiga Bancorp, TPB, TIB, Stanbic Bank, NBC, ICB, FBME Bank Ltd, Exim Bank, Eurafrican Bank, Diamond Trust Bank, Dar Community Bank, CRDB Bank Ltd, Barclays (T) Ltd., Bank of Baroda, Azania Bancorp, African Banking Corporation.

CHAPTER 5

Operating a Business—Taxation, Infrastructure, and Access to Day Care

"Women try to follow the law. Men try to evade taxes."

—Odilia Martin, Professional Cleaners
Voices of Women Entrepreneurs in Tanzania

Problems with Tax Administration

Formal enterprises of all types consistently rate high tax rates and complex tax administration among the greatest obstacles to doing business in Tanzania (World Bank 2004b). In the Investment Climate Assessment Survey of 2003, more than half of all firms rated tax administration as a major or very severe obstacle. Ninety-two percent reported they had required meetings with tax inspectors, with the median number of meetings being seven. Micro- and small entrepreneurs in Zanzibar reported fewer meetings with tax inspectors than on the mainland, and fewer requests for informal payments during tax inspections. Twenty-one percent of firms interviewed in the *2003 Investment Climate Assessment* that had required meetings with tax inspector reported that gifts or informal payments to inspectors were expected or requested, at a median value of about US$400.

The ICA observes that "the Government has increased its revenue target from about 12 percent to about 15 percent—achieving this goal will be difficult since the private sector already considers the tax burden to be excessive and tax administration is seen as corrupt and ineffective."

A range of stakeholders interviewed for the DFID/FIAS study of January 2006 noted that local taxation remains a major constraint on the commercialization of smallholder agriculture and formalization of small and micro enterprises, specifically:

- Multiple taxes (including fees and charges) make business entry difficult and expensive. Levies are perceived as exorbitant, often charged up front irrespective of the size and type of business, and sometimes duplicate a central tax.
- New charges have been introduced by local governments to replace the nuisance taxes that were abolished.
- There is a lack of transparency with exemptions.
- Coercive enforcement legitimizes tax resistance and encourages tax evasion.
- Although legislation provides that local governments are only allowed to apply fees of up to 5 percent, the imposition of other levies and taxes can add up to 20 percent of farm gate prices in certain crops in some local authorities (DFID & FIAS 2006).

Women express particular concern about the harsh way in which local government authority taxes are collected, an issue also highlighted in the MKURABITA Diagnostic (Institute for Liberty and Democracy 2005).

Problems relating to tax administration in Zanzibar include overlapping mandates and ambiguities among the roles of the TRA, the Zanzibar Revenue Authority (ZRB), and the Zanzibar Municipal Council, which leads to multiple charging of taxes, and unrealistically high tax rates, which lead to underreporting and evasion. Other issues include haphazard implementation of customs laws, and poor documentation and record keeping, which also leads to double taxation (Zanzibar Business Council n.d.).

Government Is Taking Steps to Address Concerns

In response to concerns in the private sector about high tax rates, and complex and burdensome compliance, the government has recently taken several steps to improve tax administration and efficiency in Tanzania. Tanzania Revenue Authority's Tax Administration Program, which has now been replaced with a Tax Modernisation Program (TMP), recorded successes in reforming the tax refund system, integrating its operations, and making payment of taxes possible through banks. The TMP will support TRA in delivering on its strategic goals,[1] and will provide support to the Zanzibar Revenue Board (ZRB) to implement the key activities in its corporate plan.

In addition, the Better Regulation Unit under BEST has been working to ensure that the interests of the private sector, including SMEs, are adequately reflected in the ongoing reform of tax administration, and to initiate further reforms, especially in the area of local government taxation. Important reforms that took place in 2003 were the abolition of the flat rate development levy along with other "nuisance taxes," and in 2004 business license fees for firms below a certain size were abolished. Findings of a recent study show these reforms to have reduced the tax burden on poor households by one-third (World Bank 2006c). The overall tax burden on businesses was reduced by 14 percent, with small firms paying 36 percent less tax, but microfirms paying 11 percent more tax (probably owing to stricter enforcement of business license fees).

In October 2005 TRA launched a Tax Payer's Charter, which sets out the levels of service that taxpayers can expect from TRA, and provides clear methods of redress where this service is not received. An internal evaluation of the effectiveness of the charter in terms of TRA delivering on its promises is ongoing. In the meantime, TRA continues to engage in both formal and informal consultations with the private sector on tax reform, which has had the effect of building trust between the public and private sectors on fiscal issues (DFID & FIAS 2006). Tanzania Revenue Authority also commissions an annual taxpayer perceptions survey to identify taxpayer needs, as input in the taxpayer education program.

The TRA could work to meet the needs of women taxpayers who have less education, lower rates of literacy, and fewer formal business skills than men, and who are therefore likely to find dealing with TRA challenging. Findings of the taxpayer perceptions survey are not sex-disaggregated. An assessment of its relationship with women taxpayers as part of its ongoing reform program would be helpful, as would supporting tax clinics for women, and establishing a women's desk dedicated to the provision of advice and guidance to woman entrepreneurs. As the TRA Stakeholders' Perception Survey of 2005 confirms, taxpayer awareness in Tanzania on the rights and obligations and use of taxes is still very low (NBS 2006). Yet with proper outreach and education, small businesses can be assisted to understand better the benefits of keeping records and graduating to a less burdensome tax rate.

Tax Policy Also Has Gender-Related Implications

Tax rates and administration are not the only problematic issues. Tax policy has important implications that can fall unfavorably on women. For example, the fact that Tanzania relies heavily on taxes on goods and services[2] and has the highest VAT rate in the region at 20 percent might affect women more heavily than men in that region because women tend to have lower incomes than men, and, as managers of the household consumption budget, spend a higher percentage of their income on basic goods like food. They therefore pay out a larger chunk of their earnings than men on indirect taxes such as value-added tax (VAT).[3]

Value-added tax exemptions exist for businesses below a turnover threshold,[4] although the large majority of female-operated businesses falls below this threshold. In principle they are exempted from VAT: exemptions are normally granted only to businesses that are registered. In many developing countries the registration rate for female-headed businesses is lower than for male-headed firms, partly because of time and complexities associated with VAT registration and compliance. Nonregistration by female-owned SMEs will considerably reduce the net earnings of an enterprise because they will be paying tax on higher-priced inputs, for which no redemption of VAT payments on inputs will be available (Van Staveren and Akram-Lodhi 2003).

Also, initiatives to limit deductions and exemptions can have equity implications from both a class and a gender perspective. For example, the restriction of certain deductions and exemptions that provide tax relief to women, such as childcare deductions, exemptions for dependents, or deductions for insurance and pension contributions, may create gender inequity. The elimination of exemptions on products that are primarily consumed by women, or are of primary importance to women, could also create gender bias. Relevant examples in Tanzania are sanitary items and dress fabric. In both types of taxes, base broadening, which imposes a higher burden on the poor, will also create higher burdens for women. As part of the Women's Day Focus in March 2007, the Minister for Finance announced that the ministry would review the issue of import taxes and other taxes on sanitary towels, given the burden of the tax on women.

Because taxation, with very few exceptions, alters both disposable income and the relative prices of inputs to production and consumer goods, it affects a wide range of socioeconomic decisions. For example, decisions by men and women about the time they spend in formal, informal, and unpaid work are influenced by the impact of taxation on wages and disposable income. This implies that behavioral responses to tax changes must be carefully evaluated before they are introduced, to ensure that both revenue and equity goals are met, with minimal unintended consequences. Attention to tax impacts by gender has begun only recently, but is not yet done in Tanzania.

A serious constraint to gender-differentiated tax incidence analysis is lack of data, particularly with regard to gender breakdowns of indirect taxes.[5] Information on the proportion of total tax revenue paid by women and men is not available, and gender implications of tax reform are still very underresearched. Although the links between gender equality and personal income taxes are better understood, the implications of indirect and corporate taxes still need to be investigated. More case studies need to be analyzed to give a better picture of the direction of the reforms and how they influence women. Ensuring that women, women's groups, and SME representatives are included in the tax policy and decision making process, and that they are supported in generating the data they need and in articulating their concerns, could be an important contribution to gender equity in Tanzania.

Unreliable Infrastructure Imposes a Time Burden on Women

Availability of reliable infrastructure is one of the most important components of a country's investment climate, one that greatly affects firms' competitiveness, performance, and profitability. Two areas of infrastructure, power and transportation logistics, are particularly problematic in Tanzania. In the 2003 Investment Climate Assessment, more than 59 percent of enterprises in the manufacturing, construction, and tourism sectors rated unreliable electricity supply (generation) as a serious problem.[6]

For women, the lack of adequate infrastructure for water, energy, and transport—such as feeder roads, water and sanitation systems, and energy sources, as well as the underprovision of services flowing from the systems—imposes greater work burdens and lengthens the time it takes them to perform household duties. It also reduces the time they have to participate in income-generating activities. Women are the principal gatherers of wood for fuel and water for washing and cooking, so they have by far the most substantial transport tasks in rural areas. Only 42 percent of rural households in Tanzania have access to improved water sources, compared with 88 percent in Dar es Salaam (United Republic of Tanzania 2005c). Access to basic infrastructure provides double benefits by reducing the time spent on domestic chores and the fetching of wood and water, and also by increasing the realm of small business opportunities and production activities made feasible because of water and electricity.

Access to Day Care Is Crucial

The introduction of the 1981 Day Care Centers Act, No. 17 of 1981, paved the way for the establishment of day care centers that are important for working mothers. However, conditions for the registration of day care centers are onerous:

- No person may own or manage a day care center unless he or she is a "proper organization" which is registered, that is, a parastatal organization, voluntary agency, religious organization, cooperative society, and so forth—unless the applicant has the prior written approval of the minister.
- The applicant must have sufficient financial resources to maintain those premises in accordance with requirements of the regulations and to secure "appropriate" staff.
- A day care center must have an adequate playground, proper fencing, adequate toys, materials, and equipment (prescribed in third schedule) to facilitate creative play and preparation of kids for primary education, a parents' committee, and a ratio of 1 assistant (18 years or over with primary 7 education) to 25 children.

These prescriptive and costly requirements mean that professional day care is expensive and beyond the means of most working women, and, that women rarely have the chance to own and run such centers. The act, therefore, while well-intentioned, fails to ease the burden of child care for working women. In Kenya, a recent study showed (figure 5.1) that reducing the price of child care significantly increases mothers' wage employment and older girls' schooling (Lokshin, Glinskaya, and Garcia 2000).

Figure 5.1. Lower Childcare Costs Put More Women in the Labor Market, and More Girls in School

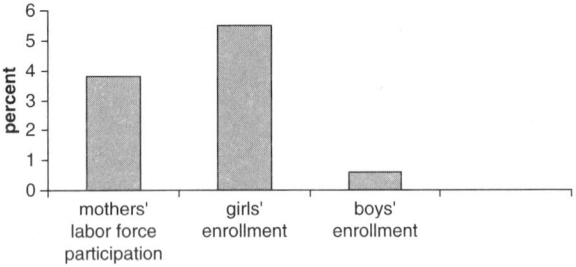

Source: Lokshin, Glinskaya, and Garcia (2000).

Key Recommendations

- Introduce special tax clinics for women to help them better understand the advantages of keeping records, the disadvantages of staying outside the VAT net, VAT and tax compliance issues, and the advantages of formalization.
- Collect gender-disaggregated data on all taxes, and the annual TRA taxpayer perceptions survey should collect and analyze gender-disaggregated data.
- Tanzania Revenue Authority could support a study on tax constraints faced by women, including its relationship with women taxpayers, and support training for women to help them overcome constraints identified. It could also consider establishing a women's desk dedicated to the provision of advice and guidance to women entrepreneurs.
- *Local level taxes:* Continue reform and streamlining of the local government tax system, monitor revenue collection in relation to service delivery, incentivize adoption of customer service culture and client charters within local governments, and encourage the introduction of penalties for use of unduly harsh and unlawful enforcement practices.
- *Tax appeals—up-front deposits:* Consideration could be given to changing this provision so that payment is based on the taxpayers' calculation of what they owe, with heavy penalties if this leads to underpayment.
- *Infrastructure:* Energy policy should focus on alternative energy sources to address the domestic energy needs of households, especially with regard to cooking fuels, and transport interventions should focus on improving women's access to transport services to reduce women's time burdens.
- *Day Care:* Reform the Day Care Centers Act on the mainland so that registration requirements are practical and affordable, to encourage more entrants to the sector and allow more women to take advantage of the services offered by day care centers. Promulgate a low-compliance-cost Day Care Act for Zanzibar.

Notes

1. (i) Improving revenue collection in a cost-efficient way, (ii) fully integrating TRA operations, (iii) providing high-quality and responsive customer service, (iv) promoting tax compliance through a fair, equitable, and transparent application of tax laws, and (iv) improving staff competence, motivation, integrity, and accountability.

2. In 2003, the share of taxes on goods and services of total tax revenue in Tanzania was 58.6 percent, compared with, for example, 36 percent in South Africa, 50.1 percent in Rwanda and 41.1 percent in Zimbabwe—DFID and FIAS (2006).

3. Direct income taxes fall more on men because of their greater access to employment and higher incomes. Consumption taxes disproportionately affect the lower-income groups who pay a larger chunk of their earnings through such taxes (Bakker [1994], Smith [2000]).

4. More than T Sh 40 million turnover.

5. Sex-disaggregated tax incidence analysis requires data on household budget management, which is rarely available in developing countries.

6. This is almost twice as many as in China (28 percent) and is higher than in many neighboring countries (49 percent in Kenya, 44 percent in Uganda). The median manufacturing firm reported outages of 48 days (67.2 days across all sectors) (World Bank 2004b).

CHAPTER 6

Labor Laws—How They Affect Women

Gender Gaps in Opportunity

Women Are More Likely Than Men to Be Employed Informally, or to Be Unemployed

As noted previously, whereas the labor force participation rate for Tanzanian women is higher than for men, only 4 percent of women are in formal employment. They make up less than 20 percent of employees in the parastatal organizations sector, and make up two-thirds of unpaid family helpers. Female unemployment has been rising since 1985 as a result of retrenchment policies, the reduced role of the public sector as a source of employment, and the declining performance of the retail sector.[1] Of the 5,684 employees who lost their jobs between 1985 and 1997, 53.6 percent were women. National indicators on employment reveal that unemployment is greater for women (4.2 percent) compared with men (2.9 percent), and is more prominent in urban than rural areas.

Gender gaps in employment also stem from norms and traditions about the appropriate role of women, which encourage households to invest less in girls' schooling or women's training (ILO 2001). In this regard, it is notable that the legal age for marriage for girls in Tanzania is 15 (and 14 with the consent of the court), whereas it is 18 for boys.[2] Women are often confined to subsistence activities at home or long hours away from home, either in self-employment or working for employers who provide little job protection or social support. Engaged in informal sector activities, their pay tends to be low and unsteady, and legal protections are not available.

Women Employed in the Formal Sector Are Disadvantaged Compared with Men

The Informal Sector Survey of 1991 and the Dar es Salaam Informal Sector Survey of 1995 showed that while both men and women were concentrated in labor-intensive, low capital investment areas, women were further pushed into activities demanding lower skills, such as local brewing and food vending, whereas men were engaged in carpentry, carvings, artistic activities, masonry, or fishing, all of which require higher skills.

When in formal employment, women are disadvantaged in terms of security, remuneration, and other benefits such as paid annual leave, paid maternity leave, and access to further training and promotion prospects. Low wages are a major source of job dissatisfaction and most women workers supplement their income with income from other activities, including sending their children to work (ILO 2001). A large number of women field workers are illiterate and few are aware of their employment situation and rights. Estate workers are particularly vulnerable.[3]

Labor Law Reform Is Ongoing

The constitution guarantees the right to work (A 22-23) and to equality (A 12-13). Employment laws also protect the position of women, and reform in this area is ongoing (box 6.1).

The critical issue for Tanzania as it reforms its labor laws is to ensure that the right balance is struck between labor protection and job security, and flexibility for employers. This is especially so in the context of Tanzania's relatively low labor productivity figures compared with its regional and international neighbors,[4] and the importance of relative unit labor costs in determining the international competitiveness of the workforce.

As in many countries in Africa, the balance in Tanzania between the need for job security and the need for flexibility is especially precarious, given the high number of underemployed and unemployed people compared with the small number of people that are actually in paid employment, and the fact that the informal sector, which accounts for about 12 percent of the employed working population, appears to be growing. Employment in the formal private sector, which accounts for about 6 percent of the employed population, generates approximately

Box 6.1

Employment Law in Tanzania

Tanzania has signed a number of international protocols with commitments to promoting employment, best practice standards in employment, and women in employment.[a] It also made a commitment at the Fourth World Conference for Women held in Beijing, China, in 1995, to address four areas of concern to women, including women's economic empowerment and poverty eradication, and women's education, training, and employment. Policies and programs to address these areas include the National Poverty Eradication Strategy, which seeks to ensure full participation of women in poverty eradication measures, and promote equality of opportunity for women, leading to a decent and productive life.[b]

The Employment and Labor Relations Act of 2004 prohibits discrimination in the workplace on the basis of gender, sex, marital status, disability, and pregnancy. It requires employers to put in place, report on, and register with the Labor Commissioner plans to promote equal opportunities. It introduces maternity leave, and contains provisions protecting a mother's right to breastfeed and to be protected from engaging in hazardous employment. A new Labor Relations Institutions Act 2004, which will regulate Tanzania's labor disputes settlement institutions, is also due to come into operation.

A National Social Security Policy that sets out a three-tier structure using various funding sources for the provision of a national social security system was introduced in 2003, and a final draft employment-based social security law has been prepared. A new Occupational Safety and Health Policy is ready to be introduced, and new draft laws on both occupational health and safety and workers' compensation are under consideration by the Ministry of Labor. A new policy and strategy on labor market information and statistics, labor market policy for employment promotion, and skills development policy, together with a draft Employment Services Bill, are with the ministry for consideration. Five new labor laws have recently been introduced in Zanzibar.

Source: Authors.
a. Tanzania has ratified all eight core ILO Conventions, including Convention 100 and 101, which are specifically against discrimination in women's employment.
b. Specific policies and strategies have been developed within the PRS. These include the *Agricultural Development Strategy* (2001), the *Rural Development Strategy* (2001), *Small and Medium Enterprise Development Strategy* (2003), the *Trade Policy* (2003), and the draft *Private Sector Development Strategy* 2006, all of which have been formulated with a gender perspective.

50,000 to 60,000 new jobs a year. Although such employment has been increasing at the approximate annual rate of 9–10 percent, this growth is nowhere near enough to accommodate the 500,000–700,000 new entrants into the job market every year, large numbers of whom will be forced into informal sector employment, where wages are low.[5] The informal sector generates approximately 100,000 new jobs per annum, a high proportion of which are taken up by women (United Republic of Tanzania 2002a).

Because of the low pay and lack of legal protections in informal sector employment, it is critical that government encourages formal employment.[6] This includes ensuring that labor standards are practical and achievable by both large and small businesses, including informal operators. If they are not achievable, the tendency within the formal sector will be not to comply with them, which leaves workers at risk. They will also discourage informal sector operators from joining the formal economy, where labor standards tend to be much higher. Costly and unrealistic labor standards tend to undermine the highly creditable objectives of labor market reform, to the detriment of wages, workplace standards, job creation and security, and the advancement of equal opportunities.

Occupational Safety and Health and Workers' Compensation Must Be Carefully Designed

The aim of occupational safety and health law is to reduce the risk of injury and disease in the workplace as effectively and cost-efficiently as possible. Unfortunately, the experience internationally is that occupational safety and health regulation based on prescriptive regulation enforced by inspections and criminal prosecution does not significantly reduce the rate of accidents in the workplace; moreover, both administration and compliance are very expensive. Most studies now ascribe an insignificant role to OSH legislation in reducing accidents, and credit technological development with the improvement of safety risks.[7] In addition, the experience with workers' compensation is that if the system is no-fault-based—in other words, employers are liable for all work-related accidents and injuries regardless of who is to blame—it discourages business owners from spending time and money making their workplaces safer.

In a 2003 ILO study women entrepreneurs running small businesses noted compliance with labor laws as one of their main challenges. Expensive workplace health and safety legislation will only add to that challenge (ILO 2003a). It is critical, therefore, that such legislation (including the workers' compensation insurance scheme) is designed to be effective in reducing safety risks in the workplace, and is affordable by employers. There is an opportunity cost attached to OSH legislation—it is recommended that options for cheaper and more effective regulatory systems be considered, such as imposing a general statutory duty of care on employers to be augmented by detailed industry specific codes of practice, which are to be developed jointly by worker and employer representatives.

Key Recommendations

- Raise awareness about rights and obligations under the laws through information campaigns, particularly on the radio
- Apply regulatory impact assessment analysis (box 6.2) to all proposed new labor policies and laws to ensure that they are effective and affordable by employers, and to ensure that distributional impacts are fair and even. Consider alternatives to regulation as well as other regulatory options before the proposed measures are introduced
- Track the impact of newly introduced labor laws, and incorporate indicators in the BEST Program's monitoring and evaluation framework that go beyond the current ease of hiring and firing, to encompass labor

---

Box 6.2

Regulatory Impact Assessments (RIAs)—Improving the Empirical Basis for Regulatory Decisions

Regulatory Impact Assessment (RIA) is a tool for improving the empirical basis for regulatory decisions. It does this by systematically and consistently examining potential impacts, including differential impacts on men, women, businesses and the poor, arising from government action and communicating this information to decision makers in a way that allows them to evaluate the full range of benefits and costs that will be associated with the proposed regulatory change. Regulatory Impact Assessment is not a substitute for traditional approaches to decision making. But, if done properly, it can make an important contribution to strengthening the quality of debate and comprehension in the decision making process. The BEST program is committed to introducing RIA as a mechanism for ensuring high-quality policy and regulatory performance that supports growth and wealth creation in Tanzania.

Source: DAI Europe (2006).

unrest, cost, and coverage of workers' compensation, costs of complying with OSH, dispute resolution costs, and maternity leave compliance rates and formal labor force participation rates.

Notes

1. The percentage of women in executive positions dropped from 6 percent in 1990 to 3 percent in 1997, and women continue to be underrepresented in all sectors, accounting for 30 percent, 22 percent, and 19 percent of government, parastatal, and private sector employees.

2. S.13 Law of Marriage Act, 1971.

3. ILO (2001) describes the housing conditions in the estates as "appalling with a critical situation with regard to water supply, sanitation, day care centers and health services." Working mothers and their babies are exposed to a number of occupational hazards including long hours of work, extreme weather conditions, heavy work loads, exposure to dust and chemicals, and insect and snake bites.

4. Analysis of the data indicates that *labor productivity* in the manufacturing sector in Tanzania is significantly higher than in Uganda but far lower than in China, India, and even Kenya. Value added per employee is about US$2,028 per employee in manufacturing enterprises in Tanzania, 54 percent lower than in China, 43 percent lower than in Kenya, and 37 percent lower in India.

5. The gross earnings for the majority of women (76 percent) in the informal sector are only a quarter of the national minimum wage.

6. This is confirmed by the fact that agricultural employment has been on the decline (by approximately 3 percent over the decade), and employment in the public sector has actually declined by 15 percent between 1990 and 2000 (United Republic of Tanzania [2002a]).

7. Regarding OSHA, see Vedder (2000)—"Summing up the historical evidence, the trends seem to suggest that, in the absence of OSHA and similar agencies, workplace safety would probably be similar to what is actually observed. The benefits of regulation, if any, are comparatively small. However, the costs are considerable."

   Mears and Chapple (1996) review a range of studies on the impact of occupational health and safety and conclude that "perhaps the strongest conclusion comes regarding regulations. United States and Canadian evidence suggests that health and safety regulations have little or no significant direct impact on safety, let alone meet cost/benefit criteria."

CHAPTER 7

Access to Commercial Justice

"We took clients to court. It was a waste of time. The court was not responsive to us. They would just say to come another day."

—Victoria Kisyombe, Sero Lease and Finance Ltd.
Voices of Women Entrepreneurs in Tanzania

Legal Mechanisms

Commercial Dispute Resolution Is Costly and Expensive

The ability to enforce contracts through the courts is critical for businesses to engage with new borrowers or customers. Firms that have little or no access to efficient courts must rely on other formal and informal mechanisms, such as trade associations, social networks, or private information channels to decide with whom to do business and under which conditions. Firms may also adopt conservative business practices and deal only with repeat customers, leading to loss of economic and social value.

Yet relying on the courts in Tanzania to enforce contracts and uphold property rights is a challenge, especially for women (box 7.1).[1] According to the World Bank's *Doing Business* database, the cost of enforcing a contract in Tanzania is well above international norms (table 7.1). In Zanzibar, recovering a US$1,000 loan through the courts takes 1,286 days and

Box 7.1

Constraints to Enforcing Justice in Tanzania

• Delays in adjudication due to case backlog, a strong injunction/adjournment culture, and old fashioned complex civil procedure rules that are unsuited to the delivery of expedited dispute resolution
• A very lengthy appeal process from decisions of the commercial court
• Human resource, technical capacity constraints, and perceived low standards of integrity, which make dispensation of justice uncertain
• Poor case reporting, which makes authoritative precedent inaccessible to judges and lawyers, compounded by poor service delivery from the legal profession
• Problems with enforcing judgments
• Suboptimal alternative dispute resolution mechanisms

Source: United Republic of Tanzania (2000).

Table 7.1. Cost of Enforcing a Contract in Selected Commonwealth Countries

Country	Time (days)	Cost (percent of debt)
New Zealand	109	10.9
Uganda	484	35.2
Tanzania	393	51.5
Kenya	360	41.3

Source: World Bank (2006a).

costs US$1,022. Appealing the decision could take 2–5 years. On the mainland, the same procedure costs US$4,745. Special "fast-track" business courts are available only to big business. Commercial courts are also available only to big business. They handle disputes of not less than T Sh 30 million, and are currently located only in Dar es Salaam and Arusha, although Mwanza will shortly come on stream.

Tanzania's suboptimal commercial justice system can reinforce a bad debt culture. A well-functioning commercial justice system allows businesses to make credible threats of court action to potential bad debtors. In addition, studies show that when contracts can be enforced quickly and cheaply, small businesses get better financial terms on loans (Qian and Strahan 2006). It is small firms—the category into which most women's businesses fall—that bear the brunt of a poorly functioning commercial dispute resolution system because they are ill-equipped to understand it, complain about it, or pay the additional fees and any bribes associated with it.

Women Face Additional Barriers in the Formal Legal System

For women, more subtle bars impair their ability to access justice. The law assumes that the parties before the court are equal, and that the courts are free from gender bias. Yet evidence suggests that women's poverty adversely affects their ability to invoke the legal machinery to seek redress, and that the attitudes of court officials are often not gender-blind (box 7.2).

The attitudes of law enforcement institutions such as the police and the courts often reinforce male power. There are cases of women who have acquired separate property during marriage who are prevented by police officers from taking it away when the marriage breaks up. In one such case in Mbeya where a wife had kept receipts of all equipment pertaining to her sewing business, the police confiscated her equipment, took her receipts and handed everything over to her estranged husband. The women was ordered to petition for divorce, whereby entitlement would be decided upon by the court (Rwebangira 1996).

Box 7.2

Hermelinda Herman v. Thadeo Mutarubukwa

A wife lived in a remote village in the Kagera Region and worked on the land, while her husband worked in salaried employment in different parts of the country. On application to the court for divorce after 21 years, the wife claimed one of the 11 developed pieces of land on which she had toiled all her married life. The Resident Magistrate made an ambiguous order that the parties should "share" the property, but did not specify how. Villages sided with the husband against the wife. They assisted the husband in preventing the wife from effecting the court order, and they caused the wife to suffer insults and ill-feeling for pursuing her claim. They did this with the connivance of the police in the region. In a subsequent case between the same parties, the high court ordered the wife to hand over her certificate of title to an urban-based property to her ex-husband. It was claimed she had "stolen" the title documents from him, despite the fact that the property was registered in her name.

Source: Hermelinda Herman v. Thadeo Mutarubukwa, Misc. Civil Case No. 25/88.

During interviews with prominent commercial justice practitioners, the issue of lack of information on the law and legal procedures, and lack of awareness of their legal rights, was mentioned repeatedly as a severe constraint on the ability of women to access justice. The problem is compounded in district, magistrate's, and high courts by complex, technical procedures for accessing the formal courts, including the fact that legal representation is required and pleadings must be filed in the correct format in English. In addition, inadequate case reporting—currently case reports go as far as 1997—means that judges often do not have access to recent legal decisions to rely on as precedent.

Fortunately, the Tanzanian Women Judges Association (TWJA) routinely collects decisions of interest that affect women and children, and ensures that judges and magistrates know about them. Other sources of support for women include the work of the Tanzania Media Women's Association (TAMWA), which routinely disseminates information to women on their civil and legal rights, as well as the work of Tanzania Women Lawyers Association (TAWLA) and NOLA in establishing and supporting women's legal aid clinics (box 7.3).

Informal Justice Systems Are Also Problematic For Women

For the vast majority of Tanzanians, the formal court system is of no relevance to their lives. Any interaction that they have with the legal system is at the level of the ward tribunal[2] and through other informal or traditional

---

Box 7.3

TAWLA: Representing Women's Rights

Tanzania Women Lawyers Association was established in 1990 to harness the energies of women lawyers in Tanzania to assist women and children who are unable to afford legal services. Tanzania Women Lawyers Association has helped thousands of women and children through its legal aid clinics to access justice. Tanzania Women Lawyers Association researches legal issues and lobbies for law reform to promote respect for human rights and gender parity, and it promotes the education and training of women lawyers. It also conducts legal literacy and education campaigns to educate society on the rights of women and children and other marginalized groups.

Source: http://www.tawla.or.tz.

dispute resolution mechanisms. However, in order for Tanzania's private sector to develop, and in order to increase access by firms to loan finance, formal dispute resolution mechanisms must be strengthened. Whereas ward tribunals may operate effectively at the level of small, informal businesses, reliance solely upon such dispute resolution methods inhibits businesses from contracting outside known networks.

Primary courts (Mahakama za Mwanzo) exist in every district, with provision for appeals to be made to the district courts. Whereas the language of the primary courts is Kiswahili, and advocates are not allowed to participate, in all other courts proceedings tend to be conducted in English, evidence must be in writing, and legal advice and representation are normally required. This makes oral contracts entered into under the customary system very difficult to enforce, since appeals must be moved from a customary adjudication system to a statutory legal system which has different courts, rules, modes of proof, and language (Kiswahili to English).

Reform Efforts Are Underway

Through the BEST program key actions include:

- Enhancing access to the commercial court and simplifying the Civil Procedure Code
- Enhancing the effectiveness of alternative dispute resolution
- Combating the injunction and adjournment culture
- Disposing of the backlog of commercial cases
- Improving enforcement of judgments
- Reviewing regulation of the legal profession

These efforts would be strengthened by the implementation of a nationwide information and capacity building program on methods and procedures for enforcement of legal rights.

Key Recommendations

- Prioritize the conduct of a gender-disaggregated baseline survey on the delivery of commercial justice in Tanzania to identify challenges in access to and dispensation of commercial justice
- Capture statistics on the numbers of female and male plaintiffs coming before the courts, the subject area of the dispute, and in whose favor the judgment was made, to identify whether perceptions about unfair

access to the courts and inequitable dispensation of justice are justified by evidence

• Support reform of the Civil Procedure Code and introduce small claims divisions within magistrate's courts, which deal with commercial cases under a certain value and are presided over by specialized judges with training in commercial law

• Establish and expand existing women's clinics (possibly annexed to the primary courts) through which women could receive ongoing education on commercial laws, legal rights, court procedures, and guidance on preparing claims and pleadings. Increase awareness among women entrepreneurs on magistrate issues

• Support routine dissemination of up-to-date case law to judicial officers across the country. Ensure translation of decisions into Swahili, and establish information centers in courts for provision of information to the public of the law and legal rules

Notes

1. The types of problems faced by the private sector were highlighted in a 1999 study by the Economic and Social Research Foundation (commissioned by the Confederation of Tanzania Industries). In a survey of 100 businesses in Tanzania, more than 70 percent of them indicated that a weak and inadequate legal, regulatory, and judicial framework affected their performance. Nearly 70 percent of respondents had used the court system, implying that informal dispute resolution mechanisms have limited relevance at least for the formal commercial community.

2. Established under the Ward Tribunals Act, No. 7 of 1985, they are widely used in resolving disputes between small traders. Membership consists of four to eight residents, known as ward secretaries, elected by a ward committee.

CHAPTER 8

Access to International Trade

*To date, studies on gender and trade have indicated that women lag behind men
in most regions in the world in their ability to gain from new trading patterns
and policies.* (Economist 2006)

Tanzania's Benefits from Increased Trade

Trade plays an important role in Tanzania's development. Opportunities
for trade expansion are critical to growth and poverty reduction. Positive
investment climate reforms, including trade facilitation policy reforms, have
augmented Tanzania's export share and investment potential. Import and
export licensing barriers have been dismantled, tariff structures simplified,
and important improvements made in customs administration.[1] Preferen-
tial import status under a number of international agreements has led to a
strong push for exports, with newly established and incentivized export-
based industries providing new wage opportunities for women.

Recently, the composition of Tanzania's exports has shifted dramatically
from agricultural dominance with the emergence of gold and gemstone
exports. Now agricultural products constitute around 20 percent of total
exports, and fish 14 percent, whereas gold and gemstones constitute
more than 40 percent of exports (table 8.1). This rapid expansion as well

Box 8.1

Trade in the MKUKUTA

The MKUKUTA emphasizes trade development toward a diversified and competitive economy:

- The National Trade Policy (NTP) will provide a guide on fostering the innovative and competitive capacity of the economy, addressing supply-side constraints, diversification of the "export basket" by stimulating value-added activities, investments in export-oriented activities, and the competence of private sector participation in regional and world markets.
- Implementation of the NTP will require recognition and exploitation of inter-sector linkages and complementary policies, including those related to infra-structure, productive sectors, trade in services (for example, tourism, transit trade) and institutional facilitation.
- Furthering economic diplomacy to market Tanzania's tourist attractions and other goods and services abroad and attract foreign investments, and for Tanzania's investors to be able to invest abroad.

Source: Institute for Liberty and Democracy (2005).

Table 8.1. Composition of Exports
(*percent*)

	1990	1995	1996	1997	1998	1999	2000	2001	2002	2003
Traditional Exports	50.2	56.2	57.1	57.8	60.5	55.4	44.1	29.8	22.8	21.4
Coffee	21.0	20.9	17.8	15.9	18.5	14.1	12.6	7.4	3.9	4.8
Cotton	18.7	17.6	16.4	17.3	8.1	5.2	5.7	4.3	3.2	4.5
Tea	5.4	3.4	3.0	4.2	4.2	4.5	4.9	3.7	3.3	2.4
Tobacco	2.7	4.0	6.4	7.1	9.4	8.0	5.8	4.6	6.2	4.0
Cashew nuts	1.4	9.4	12.8	12.1	18.2	18.6	12.7	7.3	5.2	4.0
Sisal	1.0	0.9	0.7	1.2	1.2	1.3	0.8	0.9	0.7	0.6
Cloves						3.7	1.5	1.6	0.4	1.0
Nontraditional Exports	49.8	43.8	42.9	42.2	39.5	44.6	55.9	70.2	77.2	78.6
Minerals and metals	6.8	6.6	7.3	6.8	4.5	13.5	26.9	38.9	42.5	43.2
of which gold				0.2	0.5	6.4	17.0	32.7	37.8	38.6
Other mineral	6.8	6.6	7.3	6.6	4.0	7.1	9.9	6.2	4.7	4.6
Manufactured	18.2	16.0	16.1	14.8	6.1	5.5	6.5	7.2	7.3	9.6
Fish products				7.5	12.6	10.4	11.5	12.5	12.9	13.5
Horticulture				0.7	1.5	1.6	1.5	1.4	1.2	1.1
Other	24.8	21.3	19.5	12.4	14.8	13.5	9.5	10.2	13.2	11.2

Source: World Bank (2005c).

as the recovery of manufacture exports (at around 10 percent) has led to rapid export growth (World Bank 2007a). There is concern, however, that both the gold and fishing industries are reaching the limits of expansion of natural resource extraction, with only limited prospects for future growth. This is in addition to concern about their environmental impact. A key challenge for the Tanzanian economy is thus to strengthen and diversify its export base. Tourism, for example, offers excellent potential.

Women Are Benefiting from Opportunities in Mining

Mining is one of the leading foreign exchange earners in Tanzania and con-tributes about 2.3 percent of GDP, which is projected to rise to 10 percent in 2025.[2] Recent legal and fiscal reforms have contributed to rapid growth in this sector and led to the emergence of a dynamic but fragile small-scale mining subsector. According to a study funded by USAID (Phillips et al. 2001), by 1998 Tanzania attracted the most mining exploration investment dollars of any country in Africa, US$58 million, and the activi-ties of small-scale miners increased rapidly during the 1990s. It is today the greatest single source of middle-income employment in the country, with incomes estimated at more than six times higher than in agriculture (USAID 2005). Women play a relatively small part in large-scale mining but are frequently involved in small-scale, artisanal mining.[3]

Given the capital-intensive nature of the industry, lack of investment capital for mining equipment is a serious challenge. Reduced import duties, reduced withholding tax on imported technical services, generous capital allowances, and the indefinite carryover of assessed losses create a low corporate tax burden on the sector, but these benefits are mostly confined to large corporate entities that have the financial and technical capacity to take advantage of them. Recent public outcry about the envi-ronmental degradation caused by noncompliant large-scale miners has promoted calls for more locals to benefit from the sector, but there is evidence that environmental degradation at small-scale mining sites is also a serious issue (*Sunday Citizen* 2007).

Streamlined licensing procedures have encouraged the Tanzania Women Miners Association (TAWOMA) to lobby for quotas of mining land to be allocated to small-scale women miners, increasing their share in this rapidly expanding export sector. Interviews with TAWOMA officials reveal that their members need access to lease finance, which would enable them to buy the mining equipment they need to unleash the full potential of their mines. They also need technical assistance to help them conduct feasibility studies, construct business plans and financial forecasts, and understand tax and accounting requirements, so that they can slowly graduate to the formal sector (box 8.2).

Trade Policy Is Not Gender Neutral

With imports currently exceeding exports by almost 50 percent,[4] the need to reinforce export promotion strategies has intensified. Yet it is important to be aware that trade agreements, policies, and mechanisms have differential impacts on women and men. Although increased trade offers opportunities for women's socioeconomic empowerment and growth, it can also perpetuate women's marginalization and gender inequalities.

Trade policies have encouraged Tanzania to shift agricultural production from staple foods for domestic consumption to products for export. A whole host of issues are relevant: who has access to land, which crops are considered "male" or "female," who is most likely to work on crop production and who actually receives the cash remuneration, which crops can be

---

Box 8.2

Fair Trade, Advocacy, and Limited Market Access Due to Lack of Finance—The Case of TAWOMA

With more than 300 members, TAWOMA has mobilized public and private funds from foreign and local sources for business and social investment in their areas of operation. As members of the fair trade initiative, TAWOMA members receive business development services from the Board of External Trade, SIDO, and policy guidance from the Ministry of Energy and Minerals and the Ministry of Industry, Trade and Marketing. Social initiatives undertaken by TAWOMA include education for members on HIV/AIDS, environmental protection, and child labor. As a result of sponsorship from the SME Competitiveness Facility and others to the International Trade Fair in 2005, TAWOMA members were able to market their products to foreign investors, and return with an estimated US$4.7 million in orders for Zircon and Moldavate.

TAWOMA undertakes advocacy, market research and campaigns, and fund raising and linkages for its members who own private mining companies. Through advocacy, TAWOMA members have been able to acquire legal title to their individual and group mining lands, and they now have foreign investors as partners.

Source: Authors.

grown by small or large producers, and which crops require new inputs of extensive technical assistance. Failure to pay attention to these issues may result in programs that increase exports but do not necessarily reduce poverty among the rural poor, especially women. In neighboring Uganda and Kenya, strategic exports initiatives have been criticized for creating more work for women whose labor is used for cash crop production, yet they receive little or no cash compensation, with detrimental effects on family welfare (box 8.3) (Ellis et al. 2006).

In the manufacturing sector, while the Export Processing Zones (EPZs) that provide efficient enclaves for export-oriented products also provide women with new opportunities for formal sector jobs, there have been reports of labor standards being disregarded and of women working under harsh and exploitative conditions on the mainland.[5]

Evidence from East Africa suggests that trade policy discussions tend to be restricted to a small group of insiders, where the interests of women entrepreneurs, workers, and community organizations are often not taken into account, and important information on new trade rules and their likely implications do not enter the public domain (Evans 2002). Improving the transparency of trade policy negotiations, obtaining input and feedback from the business community, including women, in policy design and decision making, and engaging in gender analysis in policy formulation would help ensure that the costs and benefits of trade reforms and agreements are spread evenly across society. Tanzania's Ministry of Industry, Trade and Marketing is very conscious of the gender dimensions of trade policy, having sent key staff to Geneva for training and ensuring gender focal points in all three departments.

Box 8.3

Women May Not Benefit from the Product of Their Labor

In Kenya, women speak of planting tobacco, an export crop, right up to their door, yet not having enough money to buy food. Women in Uganda report that government incentives to produce beans for export have left them with no food crops for their families. Poor nutrition studies show that the nutritional status of women and children is worse among cash-crop farmers, particularly where the crops are tobacco, coffee, and cotton.

Source: Maleko (2006).

Local-Level Taxes on Agricultural Production Are a Disadvantage for Women

Multiple tax systems affect women's capacity to develop agricultural activities into an export business. Whereas farmers receive favorable tax treatment because of (i) exemptions from VAT and payment of the Skills Development Levy, (ii) the ability to immediately expense research expenses and capital losses, and (iii) an indefinite carry-forward period, such benefits accrue predominantly to large incorporated commercial farmers. Smallholders pay a local government cess on volumes up to 5 percent, and the imposition of other levies and taxes can add up to 20 percent of farm gate prices in certain crops in some local authorities. Export crops are heavily taxed, in part because taxes are often levied both at points of transit, as well as at original sale. Taxes on export commodities are roughly 20 percent of sales prices. The effect is that small farmers face a higher average tax burden than do small urban businesses (DFID and FIAS 2006).

In addition to tax constraints on growth, the collapse of the agriculture marketing boards in Tanzania has created a strain on women who participated in the major agriculture value chains such as coffee and cotton. Women who used to receive institutional and extension support from the cooperative/marketing societies, particularly in the rural areas, were left to deal on the open market without the prerequisite technical skills and financial services. The result has been increased dominance of men in the agricultural value chains, reducing women's participation in many cases to that of laborers or small-scale traders of off-season products.[6]

Supply Chain Links Include Seaweed, Spices, and Tourism

Although supply chain links present opportunities for women to benefit from relationships with larger buyers as suppliers of local products, opportunities for exploitation exist. This section discusses a positive example in tourism, an example of exploitation of women in the supply chain in the seaweed sector (box 8.4), and a case study of a potential export opportunity in spices.

In tourism women are managing to establish successful linkages and benefit from the industry while delivering positive benefits for their communities, as the example of the Agape Women Group illustrates (box 8.5).

The farming of spices in Zanzibar, where women are predominant, also presents an opportunity for women to benefit from supply chain linkages. Yet although traditionally the farming of spices, vegetables, and food crops were a female domain, men have taken over the commercial production

Box 8.4

Market Access—Linkages with Private Investors Do Not Always Improve Women's Economic Status in the Value Chain—The Case of Kiwengwa Seaweed Farmers in Zanzibar

"A large private company visited our village and introduced the seaweed product to our community. The company assured us of a ready market for the product and provided initial inputs (ropes, sticks, seeds) to women's groups who volunteered to engage," says a Zanzibari woman. "Seaweed planting and harvesting is heavy, physical and painstaking work that involves carrying heavy loads of seaweed up the beach for very little return."

The output ratio of wet to dry sea weed is estimated at 8:1. Companies supporting the seaweed value chain in Zanzibar operate as a cartel, buying seaweed from village communities for a price of T Sh 135/kg of dry product. Lack of market competition and exploitative practices undermine women's profit margins to the point that they have become angry and resentful, but they are without alternatives which would enable them to break free of the poverty cycle. Fortunately, with the intervention of the Zanzibar Ministry of Tourism, Trade and Investment, this situation is being addressed.

Source: Cutura (2007).

and trading of spices, while the majority of women work as laborers. The result is that men control the income from these activities, which is not often made available for family needs. Interviews with women who have entered commercial farming and trading of spices suggest that they find it hard to compete in this market with their established male counterparts. Their niche has become that of producers with no assured markets, and their marketing option is through male middlemen who buy at uncontested low prices. Penetrating the export market for spices is even harder for women as the requirements for quality and standardization are high (box 8.6).

Women Can Be at a Disadvantage When Dealing with Customs

The bureaucratic burden associated with regulation, especially with regard to the number of inspections and days spent dealing with regulatory issues, is much higher for exporters than for those who do not export. In terms

Box 8.5

Women Can Benefit from the Tourism Industry Too— The Example of the Agape Women Group

Located at the base of Mount Meru at the house of Mama Ana, the Agape Women Group started small—with Mama Ana selling milk from cows donated by an international NGO. But with the business losing money, Mama Ana welcomed the advice of Faida, a Dutch organization that introduced her in 1997 to the notion that cheese can be made out of milk. Mama Ana attended cheese making classes at a local college, and soon afterwards was selling her product on the local market. The cheese, a novelty in the region at the time, has been a huge success that led Mama Ana to found the Agape Women Group. The group today has 60 female members who work together to produce tasty cheese and locally grown coffee. Their main constraint has been unreliable infrastructure. "There is a lot of demand for the cheese but we cannot meet it because there is no electricity here," Mama Ana says.

Taking advantage of the booming tourism industry in the Arusha region, the Agape Women Group recently linked up with a local tourist agency. For a small fee, visitors from around the world can visit the group, watch a demonstration of the cheese making process, and taste the delicious cheese and coffee underneath the shade of palm trees at Mama Ana's house. The women are using their proceeds for the good of their community—they have helped renovate six classrooms and a teacher's office in their village and have bought bricks for a hospital dispensary. They are now linking up with women in other villages, and teaching them how to replicate their model.

Source: Cutura (2007).

of customs administration, *Doing Business in 2007* heralds Tanzania as a top reformer in 2006, with delays in exporting and importing having been considerably shortened by the introduction of electronic data interchange and risk-based inspections at customs.[7] Such reforms mean that it is easier to run a reliable supply chain to deliver against promises to customers, and imply an ability to divert formerly unproductive staff time to productive business activities, reducing overhead cost structures.

However, even with large parts of the process automated, problems remain that discourage exporting and add to the bureaucratic load for compliant businesses. DTIS reports that import-export procedures in Tanzania

Box 8.6

Creating Linkages for Women in the Value Chain—
The Case of the Kidichi Spices Company in Zanzibar

A family-owned company in the spices business in Zanzibar, Kidichi Spices produces spice-flavored soaps, pickles, coffee, tea, candles, and shampoo. Their primary market is local, although through middlemen they export to Kenya and neighbouring countries. The business creates linkages with rural enterprises producing spice products. When Kidichi receives large orders from local hotels and from mainland exporters, they subcontract other women's groups in the rural areas, to which they provide training to ensure that products meet standards and client specifications. Handmade packaging using local materials is a feature that encourages the use of local materials and skills of the rural women. The group receives training from the Tanzania Board of External Trade and SIDO. Kidichi would like to penetrate international markets under the AGOA arrangement, but they need business partners in the United States who can market their products.

Source: Interview by Zahia Lolila Ramin, Zanzibar, October 2006.

are complex and duplicative, characterized by excessive documentation, repeated checking of the same information, and a general distrust of the trading community. A control mentality focused on maximizing revenue collection permeates all customs activities. The current systems and procedures employed by the Customs and Excise Department contribute to excessive delays in the processing of cargo and present a significant barrier to business activity in Tanzania and neighboring countries. Since exporting has been linked to improved productivity,[8] these barriers can have a real impact on firm performance. In Zanzibar, firms are reportedly confronted with numerous administrative barriers at points of entry and exit to customs areas when they import or export, and are required to deal with a multitude of institutions at the Zanzibar Port.[9]

For women key concerns are the potential for abuse of wide discretionary powers that women are less equipped to deal with than are their male counterparts. Even with automation, opportunities for manipulation remain, for example, in querying valuations or demanding costly extra physical inspections. Women interviewed also lamented a lack of clear information on rights and obligations, which makes them vulnerable to poor enforcement behavior by officials and poor service attitudes by tax officials. Having to hire clearing agents to assist with clearance processes is said to add to the cost of doing business by some 40 percent (Institute for Liberty and Democracy 2005).

A 2006 World Bank Urban Informal Sector Investment Climate Analysis in neighboring Kenya, which surveyed 250 firms in Nairobi and its environs, revealed that, on average, women perceive tax rates, tax administration, and customs to be greater constraints to business growth than do men. Interviews with women entrepreneurs reveal that negative attitudes and intimidation by government officials are a major issue in their interactions with civil servants.

Establishing service standards and accountability mechanisms for customs officers and ensuring that women are not treated unfairly in their interactions with officials will be an important step to encourage women to formalize their businesses and help achieve Tanzania's export growth target.

Women Are Not Well Placed to Protect Their Intellectual Property Rights

Tanzania's legislation for the protection of intellectual property rights conforms to international standards, including the WTO TRIPS agreement, and in principle provides adequate protection for intellectual property, patents, copyright, trademarks, and trade secrets. The Copyright Society of Tanzania (COSOTA) has the duty and authority to promote and enforce intellectual property rights, collect and distribute royalties on behalf of its members, maintain registers of works, production, and association of its members, and identify, publicize, and defend the rights of copyright owners. Unfortunately, with only three technical staff, it is severely challenged and underresourced. The patents, design, and models registry, and the trade and service marks registry for Tanzania are computerized under BRELA. Likewise, the Registry of Trademarks for Zanzibar was computerized in 2004.

Although intellectual property rights have been an important tool for protecting ideas, innovations, and research, they are not easily reconciled with traditional beliefs in communal property. Nor is it easy for rural entrepreneurs to obtain the expertise needed to protect local knowledge of plants or designs.

Interviews with women lawyers in Tanzania reveal that very few entrepreneurs know how to go about registering a copyright, or even know that registration is available under the law. In addition, the costs involved in

Box 8.7

Intellectual Property Rights in Kenya

Women in Eastern Kenya weave sisal kiondo bags for shopping, or to carry produce or water. These bags have been an important export for Kenya but sales both internationally and domestically have declined as buyers began to purchase imported, mass-produced imitations from South Asia where the intellectual property right for the product has been recently registered.

Source: World Bank (2007).

registering an intellectual property mark are perceived as prohibitive. The MKURABITA findings confirm that the cost and time taken to register a trademark for a new product discourage innovation. In Zanzibar it takes 107 days. In the mainland it is quicker, but registration facilities are confined to Dar es Salaam. For time-poor women who are less likely to be mobile than their male counterparts, the likelihood is they will be even more discouraged by these constraints.

Women's Rights In Music, Arts, and Entertainment Are Not Adequately Protected

With regard to copyright, women in the music, arts, and entertainment business complain about lack of enforcement of these rights and inadequate access to information on protection of innovations. The Tanzanian music industry is growing and has recently provided self-employment to youth and large numbers of women. Of the approximately 2 million paid people in the music industry in Tanzania, more than 75 percent are estimated to be women.[10] Tanzania is home to the famous "coastal poetic melodies of *Taarab*" and growing numbers of women are involved in both the *Taarab* (98 percent women) and gospel music industry (80 percent women), both of which have attracted strong international recognition.

Interviews with officials from Rulu Arts Promoters reveal that the music sector is plagued by counterfeit and copyright problems that include unauthorized public performances of copyrighted products and use of members' music for advertising, without payment of royalties. The Copyright Society of Tanzania (COSOTA), which is tasked with the collection of royalties and the legal protection of members' rights, is notoriously underfunded and resourced, with the result that despite its best efforts, musicians are being deprived of their royalties and protections.[11] COSOTA is planning to produce a national emblem (HAKIGRAM) for all the music produced by its members in the hope that this will resolve issues of counterfeit, but insufficient funding has delayed the implementation of this project.

High rates of import duty on musical instruments and inputs were also mentioned as being a constraint on the industry, as were gaps in regulations, particularly on the issue of enforcement of copyright, and percentages of royalties to be paid to musicians. Representatives were of the view that regulation in other countries provides that 10 percent of the retail price of copyrighted material must be paid over to musicians. The law in Tanzania is silent on the matter.[12]

Shortcomings in enforcement of copyright law are highlighted by the case of *Amharic* versus *Khalifan Abdulah*,[13] in which the defendant was convicted of having 200,000 CDs and 500 videotapes in his possession, for which he was fined a mere T Sh 200,000, and permitted to retain his pirated materials.

Key Recommendations

- *Trade policy development and negotiation.* Implementing gender analysis in the formulation of trade and economic growth policies and programs, and providing technical capacity-building in gender analysis for public, private, and civil society representatives, will help ensure that the costs and benefits of trade reforms and agreements are spread evenly across society. To effectively disseminate the trade policy, a popular, reader-friendly version that includes interpretation of technical issues should be prepared.
- *Export facilitation.* Conduct workshops and provide practical training for women entrepreneurs on international buyer requirements and other relevant information, to facilitate their exports to international markets.
- *Dealing with customs*
  - Specify in the Customs & Excise Management Act the limits of authority and responsibility of all officers in the customs process and institute procedural guidelines that govern the handling and disposal of goods
  - Improve access by women to information about the rights and duties of exporters and importers, customs procedures, valuation processes for duty purposes, the limits of authority of customs officers, and appeals processes

- Representation on the Customs and Excise stakeholders' forum from women in the trading community should be mandated; consultations should be regularized, formalized, and focused on receiving input from the private sector on constraints and proposed actions
- *Enforcement of intellectual property rights*
  - Embark on a widespread information campaign to help entrepreneurs understand the importance of intellectual property protection and the applicable procedures
  - Streamline and simplify registration procedures and ensure they are as low-cost as possible
  - Support sustained lobbying of politicians and the executive on the importance to Tanzania of building the COSOTA's human resources and institutional capacity to the level that will enable it to become self-sustaining
- *The mining subsector*
  - Consideration should be given to significantly extending the period of a small miner's prospecting license.
  - TAWOMA suggests that government would signal its support for small-scale mining by announcing a national small-scale miners' day to raise the profile of the industry, enable miners to get together to trade skills, and help bring media and other attention to the exploitative conditions under which women miners are working. They would also like to see support for capacity building for women miners on issues such as mineral identification, for attending national and international exhibitions, market linkage facilitation through programs such as study tours to learn best practices from other countries, and encouragement of special financing programs to support small-scale miners.

Notes

1. The World Bank's *Doing Business 2007* notes that reforms in customs administration are the main reason for Tanzania's ranking as a top reformer in 2007.
2. United Republic of Tanzania: http://www.tanzania.go.tz/miningf.html; Tanzania Vision 2025, http://www.tanzania.go.tz/vision_2025.
3. Studies show that about 500,000 Tanzanians earned their income from the mining sector during the mid-'90s, and it is estimated that women make up about 26 percent of the workforce involved in the sector. http://www.iied.org/mmsd/mmsd_pdfs/finalreport_13.pdf.
4. A trade balance of US$946.30 million was registered during 2004 in Tanzania.

5. Interview with Mary Rusimbi, TGNP Executive Director, January 2007.

6. Interviews by Zahia Lolila Ramin, October 2006.

7. The median firm in the 2003 ICA reported that it took 14 days on average for imports and 7 days for exports to clear customs once goods had reached the point of entry or exit, but some firms reported delays of as long as 50 days. Port and customs delays were considerably longer in Tanzania than in any of the comparator countries.

8. As in other countries, exporters in Tanzania are more productive than non-exporting enterprises. Labor productivity is higher and sales growth is faster for exporters than for nonexporters. Total factor productivity is also about 26 percent higher for exporters that for nonexporters.

9. Namely the Zanzibar Port Corporation, ZRB, Zanzibar Shipping Corporation, Port Health Authority, Tanzania Central Freight Bureau, and various shipping lines and clearing agents. See Zanzibar Business Council Report—*"The Role of Public-Private Partnership Linkages in Industrial Development—Zanzibar as an Illustrative Case,"* prepared by the ZBC Secretariat.

10. Interview with BEST AC Program Manager, June 2006.

11. Interviewees noted that the first disbursement of copyright royalties to the industry—an amount of T Sh 8,862,000 collected in only the first six months of 2006, was the first ever such disbursement made in the seven years of COSOTA's existence.

12. Interview with Rulu Arts.

13. Case 550, Kisutu Magistrates Court.

CHAPTER 9

The Way Forward

"We can make a big sound when we're together. The government will hear you then, and help you with what you are shouting about."

— Sarah Kessy, Afri-Youth Development Services
Voices of Women Entrepreneurs in Tanzania

Working with Partners to Bring About Reform

A National Machinery For Implementing Gender Goals Exists, But It Is Constrained

The Ministry of Community Development, Gender and Children in the government of the United Republic of Tanzania, and the Ministry of Youth, Employment, Women and Children Development in Zanzibar constitute the national gender machinery in charge of gender development in the country (United Republic of Tanzania 2005a). Within the Ministry of Community Development, Gender and Children, the Gender Division has the role of gender mainstreaming. The two ministries hold consultative meetings and have joint international missions, as well as joint reporting mechanisms and task forces for certain legislation. The ministries are responsible for policy formulation, coordination, and monitoring of the implementation of the Beijing Platform for Action. Unfortunately, their overly broad mandate, combined with the lack of adequate financial and human resources, has imposed serious constraints on the ministries' ability to implement that mandate.

Government has introduced gender focal points in ministries, independent government departments, and regional and local authorities, the role of which is to ensure gender mainstreaming in their respective institutions, as well as coordination and monitoring of gender responsiveness in these institutions. Yet their roles in practice seem unclear and their resources insufficient to meet this task. Gender focal point positions are often assigned to a junior officer who does not have the influence or capacity needed to mainstream gender issues effectively, and may be constrained by lack of adequate knowledge about how to do gender analysis. Nonetheless, the Ministry of Community Development, Gender and Children has found the gender focal points useful in bridging the gap between various ministries and the Gender Ministry, and plans are afoot to provide training and gender guidelines to strengthen their capacity and effectiveness (United Republic of Tanzania 2005b).

Within the parliament, the Parliamentary Steering Committee on Community Development is responsible for overseeing gender issues. In addition, women parliamentarians have formed a caucus, called the Tanzania Women Parliamentarians' Group and in Zanzibar, an Association of Women Members of the House of Representatives, which aim to increase awareness of gender issues in the National Assembly and the House of Representatives (United Republic of Tanzania 2005a).

One of the focus areas in the National Strategy for Gender and Development (NSGD) is economic empowerment, with plans to strengthen women's entrepreneurship skills, and facilitate access to credit and markets. The Ministry of Industry, Trade and Marketing has been active in promoting women's economic potential, both institutionally and through support for the Tanzania Women's Chamber of Commerce. Improved coordination with relevant government and private sector bodies on this issue, as well as capacity building on the links between gender and economic growth would strengthen the ministry's effectiveness in this area.

Civil Society Organizations Can Be Effective Partners

Tanzania has a vibrant and strong women's movement, with a variety of institutions addressing gender issues and focusing on advocacy and networking (box 9.1). Some of the key organizations include the Federation of Associations of Women Entrepreneurs in Tanzania, the Tanzania Women's

Box 9.1

Women's Advocacy as a Means for Creating Legislative Change

Advocacy by women's groups is important for ensuring a level playing field for women. The Tanzania Media Women's Association has been at the forefront of this effort. The association works to uplift the status of women by highlighting the barriers to their equal participation in society. Its savvy members conduct research, meetings, seminars, and advocacy through news reports and features, radio and television programs, and outreach campaigns. The pressure it has put on government to change discriminatory legislation is paying off. Working with organizations such as the task force on the proposed land bill and the Feminist Activism Coalition, the group helped change the Sexual Offences Act, and is working to change clauses in the Land Act to ensure that a man can register only one wife by law. Its quarterly magazine *Sauti ya Siti (Voice of Woman)* recently produced a special edition to coincide with a national campaign against domestic violence. The edition was launched at a highly visible awareness-raising event, which even captured the attention of the BBC and led it to run a story on gender-based violence in Tanzania.

Source: http://www.tamwa.or.tz/.

Chamber of Commerce, the Tanzania Women Lawyers' Association, the Tanzania Association of Women Leaders in Agriculture and Environment, the Tanzania Media Women's Association, and the Tanzania Gender Networking Program (TGNP) and the Tanzania Women Miners Association (TAWOMA). Although government interaction with the various civil society organizations has been effective in some cases, such as the collaboration between TGNP and the Ministry of Finance on "gender-responsive budgeting," stronger links with other civil society organizations, particularly women's business associations, will be essential for effective implementation of NSGD economic empowerment objectives.

Entry Points for Reform

This assessment recommends several changes for legal and regulatory reform, designed to increase the potential of Tanzanian women to contribute to their nation's economic growth. The BEST Program for

Tanzania is government's core program for private sector development. It aims to lower the costs of investing in, establishing, and operating a business in Tanzania by eliminating policy, legal, regulatory, and institutional constraints that inhibit a growing and competitive private sector. Imminent initiatives to engender the BEST Program provide an opportunity to profile the continuing commitment by the government to enhance the role of women in private sector development. Activities are expected to include the monitoring and evaluation of progress and outputs by gender, as well as a prioritization of reforms that have a disproportionately positive impact on the enhancement of entrepreneurial opportunities for women, including many that are recommended in this report.

Work on simplification of the business registration and licensing systems is already ongoing under the BEST Program, and given the strong support the program provides to BRELA, it is particularly well placed to champion reforms to the system for registration of personal property securities that are expected to have a profoundly positive impact on access to finance by smaller entrepreneurs, including women. The adoption of the Regulatory Impact Assessment (RIA) process as a tool for policy and law making in Tanzania, a key component of the BEST Program, offers a valuable opportunity to incorporate gender considerations and gender disaggregated impact analysis in law and policy making processes (box 9.2). This report highlights the importance of using RIA in relation to proposed new labor and social security laws that are under discussion.

Two components of the Tanzania Private Sector Competitiveness Project which aims to create sustainable conditions for enterprise creation and growth—(i) enhancing enterprise competitiveness by improving the capacity of the private sector to respond to viable opportunities in regional and international markets, and (ii) improving access to financial services through provision of support to the Financial Sector Deepening Trust— offer entry points for reforms in the trade and financial services sectors. Other entry points include the SME Competitiveness Facility, which has already provided, among other things, matching grant support for participation by women's business groups in international trade fairs, and programs such as ACCESS for African Businesswomen in International Trade, which have supported initiatives that expose women to trade fairs and provided networking opportunities for export-oriented women.

In collaboration with government and a wide circle of stakeholders, the IFC Leasing Project is already working to finalize a new draft Leasing Act which, if introduced, is expected to address many of the problematic

Box 9.2

Gender Impact Analysis through the BEST Program

"The BEST Program is currently championing the integration of engendered impact analysis in Tanzania's law and policy making procedures through delivery of widespread capacity building in the regulatory impact assessment (RIA), and the institutionalisation of RIA in government processes and structures. In addition, BEST is about to embark on a process of engendering the program, and incorporating gender-specific objectives in monitoring and evaluation plans and in project indicators and outcomes.

"BEST—Advocacy Component provides a cost-sharing grants scheme for advocacy, targeted at business associations. We ensure that women are designated amongst those who will be positively impacted by the activities we are funding. When associations bid for our assistance, they need to make a verifiable statement about this, and we monitor and evaluate that this is actually happening. We focus on women-only groups as well, and support women's NGOs. Thirty percent of our projects focus on women and the youth. Our quality assurance system formalizes our commitment to gender and comes from an understanding in our team of the disproportionately positive influence that women have on economic growth.

"Gender is a performance indicator on which my staff are judged. From the time this new workplan is in place, we will be required to report on this issue to the development partners."

Source: Interviews with Bede Lyimo, Chief Executive of BEST and Jon Burns, Program Manager, BEST AC, June 2006.

features of leasing in Tanzania described in this report that prevent it from being more widely used.

The MKURABITA Program offers an opportunity for strengthening data on land and property issues affecting women, monitoring access to land and workspace by women, land-related dispute resolution and decision making, and prioritizing reforms that support the inclusion of women on land titles. The Justice Sector and Tax Modernisation Programs are obvious entry points for many of the recommendations contained in chapters 6 and 8 of this report.

Providing the structures and entry points for women to participate freely and effectively in public-private dialogue is critical to understanding and addressing gender perspectives on reform priorities, and simplifying the message around the link between gender and growth will help remove a common perception that gender is "a woman's issue," and help to enlist the support of Tanzania's menfolk to the cause of gender equality.

Moving Ahead

In Tanzania numerous activities are under way to address gender imbalances in economic empowerment by business and civil society organizations, government, and development partners, and many are showing promising results. Key among these initiatives are (i) the engendering of the BEST Program; (ii) improved gender equity in public-private dialogue, including the commitment to include a minimum of three women in the Zanzibar Business Roundtable; (iii) the collection of gender-disaggregated statistics on access to the courts; and (iv) the launch of the Tanganyika Law Society "Gender Desk." Such promising initiatives will help to profile the continuing need for action to address legal and administrative barriers to women's economic empowerment.

It may also be worthwhile to consider the introduction of such innovations as an Equal Credit Opportunities Act, to ensure that the various financial institutions and other firms engaged in extending credit exercise their responsibility to make credit available with fairness, impartiality, and without discrimination on the basis of sex or marital status. Economic stabilization would be enhanced, and competition would be fostered among the various financial institutions and other firms engaged in extending credit by the absence of discrimination on the basis of sex or marital status, as well as by the informed use of credit. Likewise, initiatives such as the U.S. Women's Business Enterprise Policy,[1] which implements a National Program for Women's Business Enterprise (it provides that all departments and agencies are required to facilitate and strengthen women's business enterprise and take affirmative action in support of women's business enterprise), may provide some lessons for Tanzania.

Note

1. Women's Business Ownership Act of 1988, and Executive Order 12138 (44 FR 29637, 3 CFR, 1979 Comp., p. 393).

Notes on Data and Methodology for the Gender and Growth Chapter

Economic activity is difficult to measure in developing countries. First, people often pursue many different jobs, making it difficult to assign them uniquely to a specific sector or activity. Second, the definitions of economic activity as such are difficult to specify. Third, labor force participation data do not in themselves define the different economic opportunities and constraints that women and men may face. In this chapter, we have primarily used data from the Integrated Labor Force Survey (ILFS, 2000–01) to capture men's and women's economic activities. How employment is defined, and how data are collected and interpreted, raise important issues in Tanzania, as elsewhere. This appendix provides some further information on how men's and women's economic activities in Tanzania are captured, and how the linkages between gender inequality and growth are addressed.

Capturing Men's and Women's Economic Roles

As defined in the ILFS, employment refers here to people who have been working for any kind of income in any sector or type of activity during the calendar week prior to when the persons were interviewed. Paid employment refers to persons who received a wage for their work in any kind of sector, including agriculture. Self-employment and unpaid helpers include only persons from sectors other than agriculture. "Own farm" agriculture refers to self-employment in agriculture. Employment also covers domestic labor tasks such as collecting firewood and fetching water, which may have the effect of increasing the number of economically active people, and makes comparisons with other countries difficult. Unemployment considers only persons who are included as economically active. Economically inactive persons are those who are neither employed nor unemployed—that is, sick, disabled, retired, and so on. Caution is required in interpreting unemployment data, as such data generally do not capture the full range and extent of women's work (notably domestic tasks in the "household" economy), and can therefore be interpreted, misleadingly, to suggest that women have excess labor time for economic activity. More generally, labor force participation is not measured consistently and reliably, and different surveys use different, and often inconsistent, approaches. The ways in which employment data are collected and analyzed in Tanzania's Household Budget Survey, for example, provide an instructive illustration of the problem.[1]

Differences in measured LFPR between 1991 and 2001 Tanzanian Household Budget Surveys (HBS)—According to the HBS, there was an increase in the percentage of heads of households who were "not active" from 2.1 percent in 1991 to 4.2 percent in 2001. In Dar es Salaam, those reported as inactive rose from 1.2 percent in 1991 to 6.3 percent in 2001 (HBS 2002). This result is counterintuitive, since in an economy where income and earnings are generally too low, being "nonproductive" is normally considered a luxury, especially for heads of households. The main reason for this discrepancy in the data was that the question for economic activities was different in the two surveys, which would induce respondents to give different answers depending on the question and year.

The issue of main and secondary activities—The 2001 survey also asked about secondary activities, but includes economic and noneconomic activities in the same question (that is, it follows the format of the one for primary activities). The 1991 survey did not. This is clearly one reason for the decline in those reporting their status as economically active in 2001. We can see this in the cases in which the respondent had a noneconomic activity as the "main activity" and an economic activity as "secondary activity" (table A1.1). In the case of students, this was helpful, as we could more easily identify those who combine work with school: 7.6 percent of respondents answered their main activity was "student," a

Table A1.1. Main and Secondary Activities of Adults in the Last Seven Days (HBS 2000/01)

Secondary Main	Farming/ livestock/ fishing	Employed or self-employed	Unpaid family helper in business	Housewife/ household chores	Student	No second activity	Total
All adults 15–60:							
Farming/livestock/fishing	1.5	6.4	8.5	22.0	0.0	23.3	61.8
Employee—government	0.5	0.2	0.1	0.3	0.1	0.8	1.9
Employees—parastatal	0.1	0.0	0.0	0.0	0.0	0.5	0.6
Employee—other	0.4	0.2	0.3	0.5	0.0	2.6	4.0
Self-employed with employees	0.2	0.0	0.1	0.2	0.0	1.3	1.8
Self-employed without employees	0.7	0.1	0.5	1.1	0.0	3.3	5.7
Unpaid family helper in business	0.2	0.1	0.1	0.2	0.0	3.4	4.1
Housewife/household chores	0.8	0.4	0.4	0.2	0.0	6.5	8.3
Student	0.6	0.1	4.0	0.8	0.1	2.0	7.6
Not active	0.1	0.0	0.2	0.3	0.0	3.6	4.1
Total	5.1	7.6	14.2	25.7	0.2	47.3	100.0

Source: Household Budget Survey 2002 (final report), 148.

noneconomic activity. However, 4 percent (that is, more than half) do perform an economic activity (unpaid family helper in business), which they classified as secondary. The economic activity of these respondents would not be captured if analyzing only main activities, but could have been captured in 1991.

Women's economic activity—Household surveys are particularly inconsistent in measuring women's labor force participation. Not only do definitions vary across the continent, they are usually not consistent over time in the same country. In the 1991 Tanzania ILFS, the definition of economic activity excluded fetching water and collection of firewood for home consumption, whereas in 2001, as mentioned above, these activities were included. This change does not seem to have been implemented, or may have been overwhelmed by the other changes in the questionnaire. If it had been fully implemented, we would expect an increase, not a decrease, in women reporting an economic activity. However, we do see that of the 8.3 percent of women who reported being nonparticipants because they were doing housework, more than one-fifth reported a secondary economic activity.

Analysis of Gender and Growth Linkages

Gender analysis that is related to economic growth mainly rests on disparities in education and employment. An often-used method is to regress national economic growth rates on the female-to-male ratio of an indicator of education and employment or labor force participation, and add control variables as the level of GDP per capita and investment, population, and other variables common in the growth regression framework. This method has been pursued by Dollar and Gatti (1999), Klasen (2002) and Klasen and Lamanna (2003) who embed their analysis in a neoclassical growth model using panel data. Others, such as Knowles, Lorgelly, and Owen (2002), estimate a macroeconomic production function in levels of GDP *per capita*. All studies report a significant and negative impact of gender disparities in education on economic growth. Klasen and Lamanna (2003) further include the ratio of female to male labor force participation rates and a positive relation between high levels of female economic activity and growth.

Common to all studies is that they are conducted using a regression method subject to limitations that need to be borne in mind when interpreting the results. First, there are potential problems relating to the direction of causality and the measurement of variables with these types of analyses. If the positive relationship between gender equality and growth reflects a two-way relationship, or if there is an underlying common factor determining both simultaneously, then OLS regressions of income growth on measures of gender equality will not yield reliable results. Although studies have attempted to address the cause-and-effect relationship between gender inequality and economic growth, these still run into problems of measurement and statistical inference. The most common technique to circumvent causality problems is estimation using instrumental variables. This method identifies exogenous variables that affect gender equality, but do not affect growth directly, and uses measures of gender equality predicted from these variables as determinants of growth. For example, Dollar and Gatti (1999) use data on religion and civil liberties as variables that affect income only through their effect on gender equality in education. Another way to deal with the problem of causality is to average growth rates over a longer period and apply independent variables from the initial period only. This approach has been followed by Klasen (1999) and Klasen and Lamanna (2003), who use the female-to-male ratio of years of education to capture gender inequality. Although the problem of reverse causality seems to be easily tackled using panel data, the issue of an underlying variable that affects economic growth and gender inequality simultaneously is not easily dealt with. An example may be the institutional environment of a country that has been empirically demonstrated to be positively correlated with growth (Keefer and Knack 1995). Secure property rights may determine gender inequality as well as they may reflect the security of women to own assets. Another problem is due to the uncertainty of the model chosen. As the researcher does not know *a priori* which variables belong in the model, the choice of models is to some extent arbitrary. However, recent statistical advances, such as Bayesian approaches, can address this problem, although they have not yet found wide use in the growth literature.

Despite these limitations and the fact that the estimated parameters should not be interpreted at face value, it must be noted that growth regressions may still yield useful approximations provided some of the issues, such as reversed causality, are properly addressed (for example, accounting for reversed causality using panel data).

To assess the effect of reducing the gender gap in years of schooling, one may use the estimates of a cross-country growth regression which have the general form

$$y = \alpha + \beta_1 x_1 + \beta_2 x_2 + \dots + \beta_k x_k$$

where *y* denotes the dependent variable (here, economic growth rates), α and β are the estimated parameters, u denotes the error term involved in predicting current levels of growth, and the *x*'s represent the independent variables assumed to have a causal effect on the dependent variable *y*. The parameters yielded by such a model give the unit change of the dependent variable when the respective independent variable is changed by one unit. The parameter for the female-to-male ratio is estimated by Klasen and Lamanna (2003) to be 0.68. An increase of the ratio from, say, 0.5 to 0.6, would therefore increase economic growth by 0.068 percentage points. For the Tanzania case, if the ratio is increased from 0.75 to unity— that is, if perfect gender equality were achieved—Tanzania would gain an increase of growth rates by 0.17 percentage points, which is the number given in table 2.10. Referring to the problem of not increasing school enrollment at the price of greater gender disparities, one may apply an experiment again using the estimates of Klasen and Lamanna. If the average years of schooling were to be increased for boys but not for girls, this would imply a loss of growth. The current ratio would fall from 2.33/3.09 = 0.75 to 2.33/ 4.09 = 0.57. The difference between these ratios multiplied by 0.68 yields a loss of growth annually of 0.12 percentage points on average.

Note

1. The analysis of labor force participation using HBS data is drawn from M. Louise Fox, *Measuring Labor Force Participation in Africa: A Conundrum*, Mimeo, World Bank, January 2007.

References

African Development Bank. 2005. "United Republic of Tanzania: Multi-Sector Country Gender Profile." Agriculture and Rural Development Department, Tunis.

Bakker, Isabella, ed. 1994. *Strategic Silence: Gender and Economic Policy*. Zed Books, Ltd.

Barro, Robert J., and Jong-Wha Lee. 2000. "International Data on Educational Attainment: Updates and Implications." Harvard University Center for International Development Working Paper No. 42, April. Cambridge, MA.

Barwell, I. 1996. "Transport and the Village: Findings from African Village-level Travel and Transport Surveys and Related Studies." World Bank Discussion Paper No. 344, Africa Region Series, Washington, DC.

Blackden, C. M., and Magdalena Rwebangira. 2004. "Tanzania Strategic Gender Assessment." Poverty Reduction and Economic Management Network, Africa Region. World Bank, Washington, DC.

Blackden, C. M., and Q. Wodon. 2006. "Gender, Time Use and Poverty in Sub-Saharan Africa." World Bank Working Paper 73, World Bank, Washington, DC.

Bureau of Statistics. 1994. *Extension Service, Europe World Yearbook 1994*. Food and Agricultura Organization. http://www.fao.org/Gender?Static/Case St/Tan/tan-e-06.htm.

Commission for Africa. 2005. *Our Common Interest: Report of the Commission for Africa*. London.

Coopers & Lybrand. 1996. *The Investor Roadmap to Tanzania*. Washington, DC: Economic Growth Center.

Cutura, Jozefina. 2007. *Voices of Women Entrepreneurs in Tanzania*. International Finance Corporation, Washington, DC.

DAI Europe. 2006. "Consulting Services for the Introduction of a Regulatory Business Licensing System." Report by DAI Europe.

De Soto, Hernando. 2000. *The Mystery of Capital: Why Capitalism Triumphs in the West and Fails Everywhere Else*. New York: Basic Books.

DFID & FIAS. 2006. "Study of Effective Tax Impact in Five Priority Sectors." Aide-Memoire. DFID & FIAS.

Doing Business database. No date mentioned in document.

Dollar, D., and R. Gatti. 1999. "Gender Inequality, Income and Growth: Are Good Times Good for Women?" World Bank Policy Research Report Working Paper 1, World Bank, Washington, DC.

Economist. 2006. "Women in the Workforce: The Importance of Sex." April 51.

Ellis, Amanda, Mark Blackden, and Clare Manuel. 2006. *Gender and Economic Growth in Uganda: Unleashing the Power of Women*. World Bank, Directions in Development, Washington, DC.

Evans, Barbara. 2002. "Gender, International Trade and the Trade Policy Review Mechanism: Conceptual Reference Points for UNCTAD." Women Working Worldwide, International Gender and Trade Network Europe, and Development Studies Program, University of Manchester, United Kingdom.

FAO. 1997. "Gender and Participation in Agricultural Development Planning: Lessons from Tanzania." FAO, Dar es Salaam and Rome.

Forbes, Kristin. 2000. "A Reassessment of the Relationship between Inequality and Growth." *American Economic Review*, American Economic Association 90 (4, September): 869–87.

Financial Sector Deepening Trust (FSDT). 2007. "Finscope Survey 2006: Demand for Financial Services and Barriers to Access." Dar es Salaam.

Goldstein and Udry. 2005. "The Profits of Power: Land Rights and Agricultural Investment in Ghana." Working Papers 929, Economic Growth Center, Yale University.

Goldman, Tanya. 2000. "Customs and excise." In *The Fifth Women's Budget*, ed. Debbie Budlender. Cape Town and Pretoria, South Africa: IDASA. http://www.idasa.org.za/pdf/940.pdf

Gower, L. C. B., et al. 1979. *Gower's Principles of Modern Company Law*. 4th ed. London: Stevens & Sons.

Haddad, Lawrence, and John Hoddinott. 1994. "Women's Income and Boy-Girl Anthropometric Status in the Côte d'Ivoire." *World Development* 22 (4): 543–53.

International Fund for Agricultural Development (IFAD). 2005. "Inventory Study of the Micro and Small Enterprise Sector (SME) in Tanzania." Mimeo. Dar es Salaam.

International Finance Corporation (IFC). 2005. "Leasing in the United Republic of Tanzania: Market Survey Report." IFC, Dar es Salaam.

Institute for Liberty and Democracy. 2005. "Program to Formalize the Assets of the Poor of Tanzania and Strengthen the Rule of Law: (MKURABITA) Final Diagnosis Report." Institute for Liberty and Democracy, Lima.

International Labour Organization (ILO). 2001. "National Report for Promoting the Linkages between Women's Employment and the Reduction of Child Labour." GENPROM, Dar es Salaam.

ILO. 2002. "Women Entrepreneurs in Tanzania." International Labour Organization, Geneva.

ILO. 2003a. "Jobs, Gender and Small Enterprises in Tanzania: Factors Affecting Women Entrepreneurs in the MSE Sector." Mimeo. International Labour Organization, Geneva.

ILO. 2003b. "Tanzanian Women Entrepreneurs: Going for Growth." International Labour Organization, Geneva.

ILO. Undated. "Tanzania National Report for Promoting the Linkages between Women's Employment and the Reduction of Child Labor." ILO Gender Promotion Program, Tanzania.

Kalaitzidakis, et al. 2001. "Measures of Human Capital and Nonlinearities in Economic Growth." *Journal of Economic Growth* 6 (3, September): 229–54.

Keefer, P., and S. Knack. 1995. "Institutions and Economic Performance: Cross-Country Tests Using Alternative Institutional Measures." *Economics and Politics* 7 (3): 207–27.

Klasen, S. 2002. "Low Schooling for Girls, Slower Growth for All?" *World Bank Economic Review* 16: 345–73.

Klasen, S., and F. Lamanna. 2003. "The Impact of Gender Inequality in Education and Employment on Economic Growth in the Middle East and North Africa." World Bank: Washington, DC.

Klasen, S., and C. Wink. 2002. "A Turning Point in Gender Bias in Mortality? An Update on the Number of Missing Women." *Population and Development Review* 28: 285–312.

Knowles, S., P. Lorgelly, and P. Owen. 2002. "Are Educational Gender Gaps a Break on Economic Development? Some Cross Country Empirical Evidence." *Oxford Economics Papers* 54: 118–24.

Law & Development Partnership, Ltd. 2006. "Tanzania Regulatory Compliance Cost Survey: Final Report." Law & Development Partnership Ltd.: London.

Lokshin, Glinskaya, and Garcia. 2000. "Effect of Early Childhood Development Programs on Women's Labor Force Participation and Older Children's Schooling in Kenya." Background paper for *Engendering Development*, World Bank, Washington, DC.

Maajar, Rwechungura, Nguluma, and Makami. 2003. "Review of the Regulatory Implications of Business Licensing." Dar es Salaam.

Maleko, Jacqueline. 2006. "The role of women in poverty reduction and development through improved trade opportunities resulting from multilateral trade negotiations and implementation of the millennium development goals mainstreaming gender into trade and development strategies (the case of East Africa). Ministry of Idustry, Trade and Marketing. Dar es Salaam.

Malmberg-Calvo. 1994. "Case Study on the Role of Women in Rural Transport: Access of Women to Domestic Facilities." Sub-Saharan Africa Transport Policy Program, Working Paper 11, World Bank and Economic Commission for Africa; and Barwell, Ian. 1996. *Transport and the Village: Findings from African Village-Level Travel and Transport Surveys and Related Studies*, World Bank Discussion Paper 344, Africa Region Series, Washington, DC.

Mbelle, Amon, and Joviter Katabaro. 2003. "School Enrolment, Performance and Access to Education in Tanzania." Research Report No. 03.1, REPOA, Dar es Salaam.

Mduma, John. 2005. "Gender differences if rural off-farm employment participation in Tanzania. Is spatial mobility an issue?" Mimeo. University of Dar es Salaam.

Mears, Tracy, and Simon Chapple. 1996. "Government Involvement in Health and Safety: A Literature Review." New Zealand Department of Labor, Occasional Paper Series, Wellington.

Narayan, Deepa. 1997. *Voices of the Poor: Poverty and Social Capital in Tanzania*. Environmentally and Socially Sustainable Development Studies and Monographs Series No. 20, World Bank, Washington, DC.

NBS (National Bureau of Statistics). 2006. TRA Stakeholders' Perception Survey of 2005. Tanzania Revenue Authority.

NBS (National Bureau of Statistics)/United Republic of Tanzania. 2002. *Integrated Labour Force Report*.

Oxfam, Trocaire, and Concern. 2005. Report on the Proceedings of the Symposium on the Implementation of the 1999 Land Acts. Courtyard Hotel, March 2005, Dar es Salaam.

Phillips, Lucie C., Haji Semboja, G. P. Shukla, Rogers Sezinga, Wilson Mutagwaba, and Ben Mchwampaka, with Godwill Wanga and Godius Kahyarara. 2001.

Equity and Growth through Economic Research, Trade and Investment Component, Tanzania's Precious Minerals Boom, Issues in Mining and Marketing. Dar es Salaam: Economic and Social Research Foundation. http://www.ibi-usa.com/projects/tzmineralsEAGER.htm.

Pronyk et al. 2006. "Effect of Structural Intervention for the Prevention of Intimate Partner Violence and HIV in Rural South Africa." *Lancet* 368 (December 2): 1973–1983.

Qian, Jun, and Philip Strahan, 2006. *How Laws and Institutions Shape Financial Contracts*. Philadelphia: Wharton Financial Institutions Center.

Radhawa, B., and J. Gallardo. 2003. "Microfinance Regulation in Tanzania: Implications for Development and Performance of the Industry." Africa Region Working Paper Series 51, World Bank, Washington, DC.

Ramin, Zahia Lolila. 2006. Zanzibar. October.

REPOA. 1999. "Credit Schemes and Women's Empowerment for Poverty Alleviation: The Case of Tanga Region, Tanzania." Research Report No. 99.1, REPOA, Dar es Salaam.

Rutamu, I. 1999. "Improving the performance of growing heifers in coastal areas of Tanzania." MSc Thesis, Swedish University of Agricultural Sciences, Sweden.

Rwebangira, Magdalena. 1996. "The Legal Status of Women and Poverty in Tanzania." Research Report No. 100. The Scandinavian Institute of Africa Studies, Uppsala.

Saito, K., H. Mekonnen, and D. Spurling. 1994. "Raising the Productivity of Women Farmers in Sub-Saharan Africa." World Bank Discussion Paper 230, World Bank, Washington, DC.

Seebens, Holger. 2006. "The Contribution of Female Non-farm Income to Poverty Reduction." Background paper prepared for the Tanzania GGA. November (Mimeo). World Bank, Washington, DC.

Seguino, Stephanie, and Caren Grown. 2006. "Gender Equity and Globalization: Macroeconomic Policy for Developing Countries." *Journal of International Development* 18 (8).

SME Focus Magazine. 2006. "Government Urged to Hand SME-CGS to SIDO." Issue No. 003, (May–June). Dar es Salaam.

Smith, L., and J. P. Chavas. 1999. "Supply Response of West African Agricultural Households: Implications of Intra-Household Preference Heterogeneity." FCND Discussion Paper No. 69, International Food Policy Research Institute, Washington, DC.

Stotsky, Janet. 2006. "Gender and Its Relevance to Macroeconomic Policy: A Survey." IMF Working Paper 06/233. IMF , Washington, DC.

SUA (Sokoine University of Agriculture) 2007. Web site accessed on February 5, 2007. http://www.suanet.ac.tz/GPICWEB/An_overview_of_SUA.htm.

Sunday Citizen. 2007. "Mining Contracts and Revenues in Tanzania." February 25. Dar es Salaam.

Tanzania Gender Networking Programme (TGNP) and SARDC-WIDSAA. 1997. *Beyond Inequalities: Women in Tanzania.* TGNP/SARDC, Dar es Salaam and Harare.

Tanzania Women Lawyers Association (TAWLA). Undated. *"Review of Gender Discriminative Laws in Tanzania."* TAWLA, Dar es Salaam.

Thomas, D. 1990. "Intrahousehold Resource Allocation: An Inferential Approach." *Journal of Human Resources* 25: 635–64.

Tibaijuka, Anna. 1994. "The Cost of Differential Gender Roles in African Agriculture: A Case Study of Smallholder Coffee-Banana Farms in the Kagera Region, Tanzania." *Journal of Agricultural Economics* 45 (1, January): 69–81.

Udry, C. 1996. "Gender, Agricultural Production and the Theory of the Household." *Journal of Political Economy* 104: 551–69.

UNICEF. 2007. *State of the World's Children 2007.* UNICEF, New York.

United Republic of Tanzania. 2000. *Business Environment Strengthening Program (BEST): BEST Program Document, 1 and 2.* Dar es Salaam.

United Republic of Tanzania. 2001a. "Agricultural Development Strategy." Ministry of Agriculture, Food and Cooperatives, Dar es Salaam.

United Republic of Tanzania. 2001b. "Child Labour in Tanzania, Country Report." National Bureau of Statistics, Dar es Salaam.

United Republic of Tanzania. 2001c. "Rural Development Strategy." Prime Minister's Office, Dar es Salaam.

United Republic of Tanzania. 2002a. "Integrated Labour Force Survey 2000/01, Analytical Report." National Bureau of Statistics, Dar es Salaam.

United Republic of Tanzania. 2002b. "Small and Medium Enterprise Development Policy." Ministry of Industry and Trade, Dar es Salaam.

United Republic of Tanzania. 2003. "National Trade Policy: Trade Policy for a Competitive Economy and Export-led Growth." Ministry of Industry and Trade, Dar es Salaam.

United Republic of Tanzania, 2004. "Employment and Earnings Survey 2001." National Bureau of Statistics, Dar es Salaam.

United Republic of Tanzania. 2005a. "Country Report on the Implementation of the Beijing Platform for Action and the Outcome Document of the 23rd special session of the general assembly—Beijing +10." Ministry of Community Development, Gender and Children, Dar es Salaam.

United Republic of Tanzania. 2005b. "National Strategy for Gender Development." Ministry of Community Development, Gender and Children, Dar es Salaam.

United Republic of Tanzania. 2005c. Research and Analysis Group. "Poverty and Human Development Report." Dar es Salaam.

United Republic of Tanzania, 2006a. "Infant and Child Mortality Report, Volume IX." National Bureau of Statistics, Dar es Salaam.

United Republic of Tanzania. 2006b. *The Institutionalization of Regulatory Impact Assessment in Tanzania.*" Report for the BEST Program by DAI Europe, Dar es Salaam.

United Republic of Tanzania. 2006c. "Private Sector Development Strategy (draft)." Dar es Salaam.

University of Dar es Salaam Entrepreneurship Center (UDEC). 2002. "Women Entrepreneurs in Tanzania." Preliminary Report, prepared for the ILO Office. Dar es Salaam.

USAID. 2005. "Trade Liberalisation, Economic Growth and Gender." USAID Fact Sheet. http://www.usaid.gov.

Utz, Robert. 2005. *Tanzania—Recent Growth Performance and Prospects.* Background paper prepared for the Tanzania Country Economic Memorandum. May (Mimeo). World Bank, Washington, DC.

Van Staveren, Irene, and Akram-Lodhi, A. Haroon. 2003. "A Gender Analysis of the Impact of Indirect Taxes on Small and Medium Enterprises in Vietnam." The Hague, Netherlands: Institute of Social Studies. Draft paper presented at the IAFFE Conference, June 27–29, University of the West Indies, Barbados.

Vedder, Richard. 2000. "Technology and a Safe Workplace. Policy Study No. 156." Center for the Study of American Business, Washington University, St. Louis, MO.

Von Braun and Webb. 1999.

World Bank. 2000. *Can Africa Claim the 21st Century?* Report prepared jointly by the African Development Bank, African Economic Research Consortium, Global Coalition for Africa, Economic Commission for Africa, and the World Bank, Washington, DC.

———. 2001. *Engendering Development through Gender Equality in Rights, Resources and Voice.* World Bank Policy Research Report, World Bank: Washington, D.C.

———. 2002. *Gender Equality and the Millennium Development Goals.* Gender and Development Group, World Bank: Washington, DC.

———. 2003. "Tanzania Financial Sector Assessment." World Bank: Washington, DC.

_____. 2004a. *Doing Business 2004*. World Bank, Washington, DC.

_____. 2004b. "Investment Climate Assessment: Improving Enterprise Performance and Growth in Tanzania." Private Sector Development Unit, Africa Region, Washington, DC.

_____. 2004c. "Investment Climate Assessment for Zanzibar: 2003/4." Washington, DC.

_____. 2004d. *World Development Report 2005: A Better Investment Climate for Everyone*. World Bank and Oxford University Press: Washington, DC.

_____. 2004e. *World Development Indicators 2004*. World Bank, Washington, DC.

_____. 2005a. *Doing Business in 2005*. Washington, DC.

_____. 2005b. "Sustaining Shared Growth: Progress and Challenges: A World Bank Country Economic Memorandum." Washington, DC.

_____. 2005c. "Tanzania: Diagnostic Trade Integration Study." Washington, DC.

_____. 2006a. *Doing Business in 2007: How to Reform*. Washington, DC.

_____. 2006b. *Doing Business in 2006: Creating Jobs*. World Bank and the International Finance Corporation: Washington, DC.

_____. 2006c. "Local Government Taxation Reform in Tanzania: a Poverty and Social Impact Analysis." Social Development Department, World Bank Report 34900–TZ, Washington, DC.

_____. 2006d. *World Development Indicators 2006*. World Bank, Washington, DC.

_____. 2007. *Gender and Economic Growth in Kenya*. Directions in Development Series. World Bank: Washington, DC. Forthcoming.

_____. 2007a. "Sustaining Shared Growth: Progress and Challenges: A World Bank Country Economic Memorandum." Washington, DC. Forthcoming.

WEF (World Economic Forum). 2006. *The Global Gender Gap Report*. WEF, Geneva.

Yamarik, S., and S. Ghosh. 2003. "Is Female Education Productive? A Re-assessment." Tufts University: Medford, MA.

Index

Boxes, figures, notes, and tables are indicated by "b," "f," "n," and "t," respectively.